12/15/12

The Flow of Kittens

The Flow of *K*ittens

Kitten Therapy

By

Alex Zekulin *and* Patches

authorHOUSE®

AuthorHouse™
1663 Liberty Drive
Bloomington, IN 47403
www.authorhouse.com
Phone: 1-800-839-8640

Published by AuthorHouse   09/15/2012

ISBN: 978-1-4772-7127-8 (sc)
ISBN: 978-1-4772-7128-5 (e)

Library of Congress Control Number: 2012917282

All pictures in this manuscript have been taken by Monica, Katrina, or Nicholas Zekulin.

For Moni, Katrina and Nicholas.

To our family and friends who helped us out in our time of need.
You will be forever in our hearts!

A big thank you to Patie and Frank
at the Humane Society of Flower Mound.

Contents

$\mathcal{P}$reface

As I've matured in life, I've found the desire to do something meaningful, to create something of lasting value to be more and more important to me; to do something that would inspire, bring hope, or perhaps just a laugh or two. I believe I have done that here. There's been a lot of hardship all around in the last few years, and we have experienced our fair share of it. However, I believe that every cloud has a silver lining and that the glass is always half-full.

What inspired me to write this book was that hope and love come from the most surprising of places, out of the blue, seemingly when you need it most. It can radiate out and fill your life and those around you with joy in many unexpected ways. Our experience told here recounts that hope and love. Perhaps it's one indication of how God works in our lives. I hope this book brings you some joy, because then I have done some good. We have many kindnesses to return, for all of the good deeds and help we have received from so many people over the last few years. To that end, this book is my start.

Alex Zekulin
Flower Mound, TX
September, 2012

I just want better tasting cat food for my family!

Patches

Alex's Tale

1 Kittens on the porch!

Patches, you're such a crazy nut! I laughed as he jumped on me, startling me to full attention. I was sitting relaxing on the couch after a hard day when, out of nowhere, Patches jumped on me. He does that a lot. I do believe that he was smiling at me. Cats have that way about them sometimes. Patches settled down on top of me. Suddenly, I had my own little heating pad, a warm comfortable kitty sitting on me on a cold winter's day.

As I looked at him curled up, purring, with a content look on his face, I couldn't help but think back to the day when Patches and his brothers, sister, and mother came into our lives. Little did I know the affect that one event would have on *our* lives, as well as theirs.

It was September 2009. It hadn't been a good year for our family. Like many other families, ours was affected by the economy. I was laid off after eighteen years. No one was hiring, or if they were, I was competing against 100 other folks in the same boat. After ten months of this, our patience and finances were wearing thin. It seemed that everywhere we looked, there was nothing but bad news, with no end in sight.

That evening, in September, Nicholas, our nine-year-old son, came running into the house, shouting something about kittens in the bushes in front of the house. He was sitting in the front yard with his friends, Evan and Erin. They heard a noise in the bushes and suddenly saw some tiny kittens playing. One of them, an orange and white kitten, poked out from behind the shrubs, looking at the strange small people looking back at him.

After everyone went home, we happened to notice the furry little kittens running around on our porch. They were so cute! Mom was there with them, keeping an eye on her little ones. We had two cats of our own, Koko and Tigger. Now we finally realized what they had been so intently looking at out the front window for the last two weeks. They were watching Momma cat and her kittens. They had been here for a while. It was dinnertime; so naturally, I went to the cat's cupboard and opened a can of cat food and found a spare bowl. And, of course, they had to have water to wash it down with, too. As soon as they heard me opening the door, they vanished into the bushes.

I put out the food and water, right in front of the front window. I could hear the rustling of the branches in the bushes as little eyes peered intently at the big scary man. As I stepped inside, they reappeared out of thin air, pouncing hungrily, surrounding the bowl. You would think they hadn't eaten in days! We all stayed glued to the window, watching them eat, then play! We would easily spook them through the window, so we peeked around curtains, through the glass in the front door, and anyway we could. There was laughter in the air. We were smiling. And oh how we needed it.

I'm pretty sure I heard the question asked that first night, the first of many times, "Can we keep them?" So let me tell you about them. Momma is a calico. And that endeared her to us right away. Our first cat, our first baby, was a calico named Honey. We had her for many years. She went on trips with us. We took lots of pictures of her. We coddled her like any first-born child. You get the picture.

So mom cat, or Momma cat, as we now call her, is a loving and doting mom, carrying her kittens, and making sure all was okay. She was protective of her brood and made sure I felt threatened when I approached them. She would hiss and then meow when I brought out the food. The kittens were a cute mix of gray, white, and orange, calico colors, but not all in one cat. Patches is a gray and white tabby with a distinctive tabby "patch" of color on his face. Mickey is similar in color, but with no patch on his face. Instead, he has a beautiful white furry face, with a *really* pink nose. Sabrina is a dark gray tabby, all gray. Apricot, or Appy, as we like to call him now, is an orange white tabby mix.

Now, when we started this adventure we didn't know their genders, and their names changed over time, but I'll cover that later. The only thing we knew about them was that they were very cute. And they were very hungry. We watched them for days; they would come out in the evening after we put out food for them. We worried about them when they didn't show up for dinner or breakfast. We were now feeding them twice a day. If one was missing, that was cause for great concern in our whole house.

And speaking of our house let me introduce ourselves. I'm Alex, the husband and dad of the house. Monica is my wife and loving mom to Katrina and Nicholas. Katrina, our oldest, is now nineteen now, but was sixteen when all of this was going on. Nicholas is our youngest. He's twelve now, but was nine when this story started. Oh yeah, how could I forget, Koko and Tigger. Koko is our oldest cat; he's now about eleven and is a snowshoe tabby. That means he's a tabby colored cat, with four white "snowshoe" paws. Tigger is about eight and is a gray tabby, a pretty "Russian blue" sort of gray with soft fur.

Let me tell you a little about Koko. He was probably a dog in a previous life. When our doorbell rings, he growls, his fur goes up, and he protects the home. He hangs around with us and loves to be around people; not *on* people, but around them. Tigger is the polar opposite. The doorbell rings, and there goes the gray flash, under our bed. But he has a wonderful personality, very lovable, on cat's terms, and loves to sleep with us, sort of like a second pillow. We got Koko when Honey was getting old. She was still feisty when it came to the new kitten in her life and made his life difficult with lots of hissing.

She passed on about a year later, just after Nicholas was born. After a couple of years, we decided that Koko needed companionship, so we adopted Tigger. We gave him the name because he bounced around like a famous Tigger from storybooks. Of course, he was gray, but that didn't matter. The two cats tolerated each other's company, then became friends. They would often be sitting around us in the evenings as the family watched TV.

Now both of them were behaving strangely, constantly running to the front window and the front door, especially in the evenings. We looked, but never saw anything; not until Nicholas and his friends saw the kittens that day. From that point on we couldn't keep our eyes off them.

We spent many hours watching them play, sleep, eat. That's pretty much it. But they were so cute! I put a computer camera by the window and started to record their adventures on our porch. You can see these videos on our website, www.flowofkittens.com. I saw an old playhouse of Koko's that was gathering dust in the corner. It was a soft-sided foam stuffy cube playhouse, with two large round openings.

We put it out there for the kittens to play in. They loved it, especially after a nice meal.

They could play for an hour, jumping, pouncing, and wrestling in and around the cube. At first, they were too small to move the cube much, but pretty soon they were pushing and shoving it as they played in and on top of it, then, suddenly, they would fall asleep, many times in the cube, or on the cube, especially if the sun was shining on it. It was toasty! Watching the kittens brought much needed joy to us that fall. It was uplifting. With the heartache and pain we had suffered and were still suffering through, they were an incredible joy to watch.

When one of them was missing, the worry we felt would only go away once we saw the missing kitten again. Of course, we started naming the kittens. I chose Patches for the kitten with the patch on his face. The name stuck. Nicholas named the orange kitten Lilly, because "she" was a cute kitten, and we liked the name Lilly. We later learned that Lilly was a boy, and that orange tabbies are all boys, kind of like calico cats are all girls. So later Lilly became Apricot. We didn't name the gray kitten right away. We did think "he" was a boy. And Mickey was the other gray kitten mix, the one without the patch; he got his name later, too. For now they were the gray kitten, and the gray and white kitten, without the patch.

I called the Humane Society of Flower Mound (fmhs.org) to ask what options were available to us, as far as the kittens were concerned. I talked with Patie there, who not only took a personal interest in the kittens, but in our family as well. It's amazing the kindness that flowed toward our newfound charges and us. The upshot was that if we wanted to help the kittens beyond just feeding them, we'd have to be proactive, to take charge of the situation. We'd have to catch them! Remember, these guys could disappear into thin air at just the sound of the door being unlocked. Once they were caught, the option was ours to foster them or hand them over to the Humane Society for fostering.

Patie provided us with traps to catch the mother and her kittens by luring them into the cages with food. I never understood how they did it, but the traps never sprung, at least not for Momma and her kittens. I did catch an opossum. I have a video of him visiting the kittens' food bowl. We did catch two other cats, both males, who are probably the fathers of the kittens; more on that later. But I never caught the kittens.

Either the food was eaten and the trap not sprung, or the food was ignored. Patie also provided us with a nice large cage with a cat carrier and litter box to put the cats in when we caught them. We set it up in the garage. Wait, there's a story here.

I watched from my office window, recording their every move on my PC's camera. I agonized over the capture of the kittens and what would happen, how would it go over, and would everyone be all right. The plan was to catch Momma and her kittens. I procrastinated for weeks. Watching them out the window was all I would do, outside of feeding them twice daily. One of the videos we captured was of a visiting opossum. He or she was eating the food we put out for the cat. When we noticed it, we got pretty scared, thinking it had killed or hurt the kittens. You can see me chasing it away on our website.

They really loved that cube, pouncing, bouncing, and rolling it around, sometimes with another kitten inside. Sometimes they would sleep in there. Momma would be nearby, and at other times she went about her business. Finally, the opportunity presented itself. As I watched the kittens, three of them had fallen asleep inside the cube. It was time to take action.

I watched them play, then fall asleep. I would have to settle for three out of four. I would lure the other with the trap. I went from my home office into the garage. I made sure the big cage was ready. I left the main garage door open. I setup the garage's remote control near the cage and then walked outside quietly around the front of the house, to the door and the front porch. I took off my shoes and tiptoed onto the porch. I peeked around the corner; there was the cube! I snuck up to the cube and quickly snatched it, collapsing the cube around the openings to block the kittens inside.

The kittens at first weren't moving, but a few seconds later they went nuclear. I held the collapsed cube tightly in my arms as I rushed around the side of the house into the garage. I got the door closed (thankfully), then loosened my grip slightly and opened one of the cube's holes and pointed it into the open cage in the garage. As soon as they were out of the cube and inside the big cage, I closed the cage door.

Now, if you ever imagine where the expression great balls of fire could come from, I've now got an idea. The kittens flew out of the cube and into the cage. They ricocheted all around the inside of the cage, bouncing, climbing, crying, and in general letting me know that this was unacceptable. I soon discovered that there were four kittens in the cage. I did it! And as quickly as that thought sunk into my skull, one of the kittens (one of the gray and white ones) found an opening in the cage and squeezed himself through it. And then he was gone, somewhere in my garage.

Now, for most normal people, their garage is a neat organized place, with not a lot of places for a tiny kitten to hide. This is not the case in our house. Let's just say it's the ultimate hiding place for a tiny scared kitten. Once I realized how the kitten had gotten out, I blocked the two openings with my hands. This worked, but I couldn't do this for long, plus I had to find the loose kitten before he hurt himself. The openings in the cage were gaps designed to allow the cage to collapse easily for transport. For a normal sized cat, this wouldn't make any difference. But for a tiny kitten, this was a chance at freedom.

I moved the cage against one garage wall, closing off one opening. Then I found something to put against the other side, all the while pushing kittens away from the hole. At least they were now secure; I hoped! Now I could focus on the lost kitten. Needless to say, he didn't want to be found. I searched everyplace I could think of in my garage, behind shelves, my workbench, boxes, bins, etc. I was worried about the sharp saws on the floor in the garage. I moved them and decided to look behind a shelf that was on the floor, leaning against the wall, under the sink. There he was!

I had to act. I reached in and grabbed him by the scruff, or as best as I could do. I scruffed him, picked him up, and quickly ran to the cage. Remember the great balls of fire? The kitten, whose fight or flight instinct kicked into overdrive, attacked what was attacking him. That happened to be my hand. He drew first blood. I managed to get him into the cage and close the cage door. I had done it! I captured the kittens! I was bleeding, pretty badly, but I had done it.

The feeling of elation, of having achieved a significant accomplishment, suddenly became what do I do now. I remember feeling the same way after Katrina was born. The incredible joy, excitement gives way to what do we do now? I remember the doctor asking us, just before we were to leave the hospital with our newborn daughter, do you have any questions? Uh. Yeah. What do we do now? Same here. Thankfully, that's where Patie comes in.

Patie volunteers at the Humane society of Flower Mound. She's the person I talked to when I called for advice on what to do with the kittens in our yard. She provided us with knowledge, sage advice, and the trap and cages to catch the kittens. I called Patie in a panic when I first got the kittens into the cage and one of them escaped into the garage. She said she would come over and help find the lost kitten. When she came over, I showed her the captured crew. They were huddled up, frightened, in the smaller cat carrier in the large cage. She gently talked to them, reassured them in a calm voice. They were so scared!

It was decided that we would have to move the cage from the garage into the house. But where to move it to? The cage was big and unwieldy, and we wanted to keep the kittens away from our two older cats. Patie brought us a large carrier; the kind big dogs travel in. We placed the smaller carrier with the kittens inside the big carrier. This was our view. From left to right, are Apricot, Patches, Mickey, and

Sabrina. We tried to find a place in the house where we could keep the big carrier. This wasn't a simple task. We tried all sorts of places to put the large carrier, the half bathroom on the first floor then out in the hallway. Nothing worked well.

Meanwhile, Patie checked each one out, gently scruffing them and checking their gender and general well being. By her tally, we had three girls and one boy. The next day, Frank, a fellow HSFM volunteer, brought over some medicines for the kittens. First he gave them a dab on the back to de-flea them, then some yummy medicine to de-worm them. That had gone smoothly.

The kittens were in their tiny carrier, which we placed on top of the big cage. This is probably my earliest recollection of the kittens' individual personalities. Patches was the easiest to grab. He was the bravest. Frank grabbed him, gave him his medicines, sexed him (boy), and gently plopped him into the cage. Next came Lilly. After Frank was done, Lilly became Apricot. Next was the future Sabrina. As Frank reached in, Sabrina took exception to his hand and let him know it. She drew blood from both of us! She did get her medicine, but didn't have her gender checked. She's a proper lady! However, this earned her the nickname Venom. Frank and I spent the next few minutes stopping our bleeding and bandaging ourselves, applying antibiotic ointment, and wiping our blood off the floor.

After a brief chance to recover, we tried to grab Mickey. He hissed big time, so we gently dumped him from the carrier to the cage without checking his gender. He did, however, get his medicine. At this point, Frank determined that we had three boys, maybe, plus one unknown. It was a rush job, but we were sure about the orange kitty and Patches. That was when Lilly became Apricot, Patches was Patches, Mickey was called Hissy, and Sabrina was called Venom.

Katrina came to the rescue. She suggested our hall walk-in closet as a location for the cage. It was big enough, and would provide the seclusion the kittens needed, as the rest of the house was open to our two cats Koko and Tigger. I emptied the closet. We had a lot of stuff in

there. We moved the cage to the closet and let them into it. It had more room, food, water, a nice bed, and a litter box. What a busy day!

The kittens got a lot of handholding time with us. We would each spend hours in the closet holding them and letting them explore the closet and the outside of the cage. We were coming in and receiving "kitten therapy." It started in the closet with hour-long sessions. We continued it even after we moved the kittens out of the closet. The therapy was beneficial to all involved, kittens and us. So much time was spent looking at cute kittens falling asleep in our arms. It was a truly wonderful experience.

But every night, they would be back in the cage, and we would close the door. This scenario worked for a week, maybe two. But the kittens were isolated, didn't see the sun, and we could all see that this wasn't the right place for them. Patie suggested that they should interact with us more and see us as we moved about the house. They were adapting well, but Patie wanted a better environment. She asked

if we were sure we wanted to foster the kittens. Frank, the fellow HSFM member who brought the medicines for our kittens, also fostered many feral cats, and said he would be able to take them.

When I think back, this is the moment that changed our lives and that of the kittens forever. At this point, the feeling of having such incredible joy in our lives being interrupted, or removed, wasn't an option. This is the second time I remember hearing, "Can we keep them?" We politely declined the offer to have Frank foster them, and instead decided to foster them ourselves. We had swallowed hook, line, and sinker. We gave them their names! In hindsight, this was the tipping point.

Patie and Frank to the rescue, again! Patie arranged for us to meet with Frank again, this time to borrow his special cage for our use. The next day Frank arrived with his cage. It was a huge upgrade. Frank is a wonderful man whose love for animals is only exceeded by his love of people. His charm and folksy wit is disarming. I was so glad to see him.

Frank brought the cage over in his pickup truck. He had built the cage himself. As a result, it had many desirable features. First, it had a detachable floor. Second, it had multiple sitting levels with padded beds and perches to sit on. Third, it had two doors, one on the bottom, to change the litter, the other above to access the upper part of the cage. Last, it was roomy enough for the kittens, and it had lots of neat hanging toys to bat around and play with. A kitty condo! Oh yeah, it had wheels, too. We wheeled into our house and promptly stopped. We wanted to have a central location, with access to daylight and the convenience of being able to move around the cage. Conveniently, the cage was already in the optimum location; our foyer! We washed the now famous cube and attached it to the inside of the cage.

The kittens were now in their new home. It was a definite upgrade; a condo with a view! There was a lot to see and observe and nice sleeping arrangements. Our next-door neighbor Mary brought over a little house for kitties. It was about two feet tall and had two levels, with a neat hanging bed to lie in.

It was closed from one side and open on the other with holes for kittens to run through. This let the kittens have two hideaways in their new home. But the best part was all of the new toys that were just hanging from the top of the cage. Why, a kitten could play all night! They came alive in their new home. And played late into the night, they did.

The kittens adapted to their new home, but they were still very and frightened of us, especially of our two cats. There was some hissing as Koko and Tigger passed the cage to check out what the people of the household had done to their lives. The kittens loved to play in their condo. They would bat the toys, climb the cage, race inside and out of the cube, and leap up and down levels, then either stop to look at the cats, or us, then fall asleep on a bed, in the cube, or even on top of the cube.

Around this time, I went away on a trip for about ten days. It was November, cold and dreary where I was. I missed my family and our new kittens very much. Then, I got a wonderful surprise; an email with pictures from home! Monica had taken pictures of Nicholas playing with the kittens, as I was talking to Nicholas on the phone. Here he is with all four kittens! That was a first.

Monica was excited as well. She had gotten Mickey out of the cage and was holding him, alone. He settled down on her chest, feeling her heartbeat. She told me how he wanted to escape at first. But she managed to calm him down and lull him to sleep. Truly a first!

By the time I had returned from my trip, there had been an incredible transformation in the kittens. This is when their personalities first began to really stand out and shine. Patches was the brave kitten who always wanted to be held and taken out of the cage at anytime. Apricot was usually next. He would come out, but be a little

more reserved. Sabrina was shy, but could be grabbed. She wasn't happy, but would soon settle down in our arms. Mickey was hard to catch, and did his best to keep from being held. But he has the cutest pink nose. Oh, by the way we had three boys, and one girl!

We enjoyed the kittens immensely. Patches was out in our hands every chance he could. Since he was the first to the cage door, and since I was usually around, he and I got to spend some quality time together. I could feel my heart slowing down, my body relaxing, and my soul calming down, as I held a kitten in my arms. Watching a kitten fall asleep in my arms was magical. This made for a topsy-turvy Christmas. On the one hand, financially we were in ruins. On the other, we had our health, our family, and warm fluffy kittens to make our days. We had a lot to be thankful for, but didn't appreciate it yet.

Now, we hadn't forgotten about Momma cat. We continued to put food out for her. I could tell she was agitated whenever I saw her. I don't know if she saw me take the kittens. I'm sure she could hear them, first in the garage and probably in our house. Nevertheless, she always kept coming for food. We tried to capture her in the trap, baited with cat food. She always managed to eat the food without setting off the trap. We succeeded in capturing another potential father to the kittens, but not Momma. I finally gave up trying to catch her and just gave her food and water. We tried to put some blankets out for her, and even gave her fresh warm water every day in the winter.

Later, I put a replenishing water bowl for her in the summer so that she would have fresh water. Patie had advised us that Momma had probably moved on from the kittens pretty quickly. Apparently that's their way; I wasn't sure. To this day, when I feed her, she gives me a hiss, then a gentle meow. The hisses seem to be getting shorter and the meows longer. Someday, I hope to pet her.

The kittens were in their cage for Christmas. Although they spent many hours out of the cage a day, being held and exploring the house some, they were quickly outgrowing the cage. A better solution needed to be found. Frank was a source of wisdom. As I was deliberating about keeping the kittens, Frank opined to me, it's not who you're going to keep; it's who do you send away. Who do you reject? If you search your heart, this is true. Each of us had a favorite, and a second, and could easily provide a good reason for why we should keep one, two or thee and yes, of course even all four kittens. But when we asked whom do we give away, even to a loving home; the answer was a deafening silence. The thought of seeing one of our kittens in a cage being put up for adoption was unbearable. The kittens had found a

home, and we were it! Of course, we weren't in any financial position to keep them, but that was something to be dealt with later.

Finally a New Year had arrived. Here's hoping 2010 is better than the horrible 2009. Well, I guess it wasn't that bad; we did find the kittens. This gives credence to the expression "every tragedy has a silver lining." So it seems.

Now came a fun part. Where to move the kittens? We deliberated as to which room would be best. For a number of reasons, we settled on Nicholas's room, mostly because he wanted them more than anybody else. We started to "kitten-proof" his room. This involved taking everything that a kitten would want to play with, and shouldn't, then anything that they would break, and finally putting down a plastic tablecloth to protect the carpet, then a place for food and a litter box. Once we were done, it was time to migrate the kittens.

2 Nicholas's Room

We each picked a kitten up and out of the cage, and carried them off to Nicholas's room. They were curious. It wasn't often that we would grab all four, mostly because Mickey was getting more difficult to catch. He'd developed his aversion to being held. Once we were in Nicholas's room, we closed the door and let them go. It was fun to watch them. They walked around, exploring his room, under the bed, the windowsill, the desk, and his dresser. Every nook and cranny had to be checked and rechecked. I had put in a new litter box that was covered. We placed it on the plastic tablecloth, to keep the carpet clean. Last, I couldn't resist. Nicholas and I bought them a climbing perch, one of those multi-level cat scratching, climbing, carpet-covered things; a multi-level carpeted cat-climbing structure. We placed this by the window, giving the kittens a bird's-eye view of the birds in the tree right outside of the window. Whenever we came home, we would see a kitten sitting on the windowsill, sunning.

The kittens had been in Nicholas's room individually during their explorations of the house, but they were supervised. Here they had a room with a view, afternoon sunshine, and a warm sunny bed to sleep on. The kittens soon discovered the trundle bed under Nicholas's bed. It was the perfect place to hide, sleep, and play. In hindsight, it just occurred to me why they all liked dark places. Before we caught them, I assumed that they "lived" in our bushes when they weren't on our porch playing, but they probably spent much of their time in our local sewers. There they were relatively safe from people and dogs, and since they were underground, it was cooler when it was hot, and warmer in the winter.

When they were alone, Sabrina and Mickey liked to stay on the trundle bed. Patches preferred to stay on top of the bed, in the open daylight. Apricot loved the window. Actually they all did, especially when it was sunny. Slowly, they all grew accustomed to the room and loved when we visited which for me, was often, several times a day. I would spend my days sending out resumes, applying for jobs online, calling network contacts and scouring the web for open positions. And when that grew too frustrating, I would go up to Nicholas's room for some loving. The kittens loved when we were with them. We had succeeded in domesticating our feral kittens.

Some of the fondest memories I have of the kittens are of our quality time in Nicholas's room. I would come into the room, close the door behind me, and be surrounded by kittens. I'd sit on the floor with my back against the wall and would have instant gratification. Patches would quickly climb onto me then plant himself on my chest or shoulders. Sabrina would sit on my upper legs or thighs. Apricot would plop onto my ankles, and Mickey would sit just outside of arm's reach, purring loudly. They would all purr loudly. Sometimes I would lie on the bed and be covered in kittens. Patches and Sabrina would quickly climb onto me, and make a nest on top of me. Apricot would climb on my legs, and Mickey would sit just outside of arm's reach. Sometimes he would let us pet him. He would purr, but was uneasy.

Nicholas's room faces west, so his room got lots of afternoon sun. The sun would shine perfectly onto his bed; purrfect for kitten sunbathing! I would often find the kittens lying on the bed, sunning themselves or sleeping. It was so nice to snuggle up and have kittens pile on top.

As time went on, it was more difficult to sneak in and open the door without kittens knowing about it and intercepting me. It got to the point where it was easier to open the door and let them run into the adjoining playroom, which had its own door, that, when closed, blocked access to the rest of the house. In the playroom they would climb on the shelves, explore the boxes from Nicholas's room, with items that were cat proofed from his room, and in general, they could play. Because the room was a mess we worried about the kittens getting hurt, or eating something they shouldn't. Occasionally, Koko or Tigger was in the room, and they would get a chance to see each other eye to eye.

Unbeknownst to me, one of the kittens' favorite activities was to peek under the door into the playroom and play under door tag with Koko and Tigger. Once we moved the kittens into Nicholas's room,

Koko and Tigger figured out where they were and would peek under the door, which was now always closed. Before that, the two cats had free reign in Nicholas's room, especially Tigger, who loved the sunshine and sleeping in Nicholas's bed.

Now the way was blocked, and those annoying kittens were on the other side of the door. Tigger was jealous of the kittens in general. But when we moved them into Nicholas's room, I think it affected him more so than Koko. Tigger mushroomed or perhaps ballooned into a gray Garfield. Although he was still spry, we couldn't help but notice his newfound paunch.

It was cute to watch them play tag with each other's paws under the door. This could go on for the better part of an hour. First patches, then Apricot, then Sabrina and Mickey; all couldn't resist the paws from the other side. It was fun to sit in the room and watch them play. And, of course, anything that we should have kitten-proofed, but didn't, was tested by the playful gang. This included brushes, night-lights, dry cat food, toys; nick-knacks that we thought were safely out of reach, all were there for the kittens' amusement.

This is probably a good spot to stop and mention an important principle in all animal care, but especially with more than one cat. What goes in comes out. In my opinion, the litter box is the most important item for our cats. When I was little, we had a pet raccoon that we toilet trained (a future book perhaps.) Unfortunately, our cats require a litter box. Actually, they require more than one. I really wish I had toilet trained them!

This is probably the single most annoying thing about having so many cats. The litter box needs to be cleaned daily, at a minimum, and probably twice a day to be perfectly honest. I've yet to find an automatic one that can handle the workload. I'm willing to take on the challenge of testing them if a vendor wants to put their claims to the test. Believe me, I've burned and shorted them out. There are websites and common interest forums dedicated to automatic litter boxes. I'd like to be able to let those folks know that a particular model rose to the challenge.

Anyway, the kittens grew in Nicholas's room, both physically in size and emotionally, in their attachment to us. We all loved to take turns or go together into Nicholas's room to play. If we were looking for one of our family members, chances are they were in Nicholas's room getting some quality time with the kittens.

It was here in Nicholas's room that we got to see the kittens' personalities emerge. I already mentioned that Patches was the brave one, who quickly ran to us when we came into the room. He's the alpha kitten of the group. He's the first to check new things out and usually the one the others watch to see what happens. Patches simply loves to be with us. He can sit on us for half an hour, initially purring up a storm, then falling asleep in our arms, or on our lap. Another thing that's curious about these kittens; they will look us in the eyes as if trying to communicate. I grew up with lots of animals in and around the house. Most of the animals will look me in the eye, but then turn away, especially a cat. Patches especially, and even the other kittens, will look me in the eye for some time and meow as if asking a question. It's touching.

I did notice that Patches is the most dynamic of the kittens. He's always there in the middle of the action, whether it's simply being with us or playing with his brothers and sister. I can count on him being in or near the action. He probably causes most of the play fighting by stalking and pouncing on his siblings, but they don't seem to "fight" for long, but rather roll around for a few seconds and move on. He'll

be the first into the bathroom or the closet, and will definitely be in the lead when food is served, followed closely by Apricot.

Sabrina, aka, Venom, is the kitten who has grown the most as far as adjusting to her new home and to absolutely loving us. As I mentioned before, we nicknamed her Venom because of her attitude toward being kidnapped and being taken from her mother. While in the cage in the foyer, she would like being held sometimes, but usually hid, along with Mickey. Toward the end of her tenure in the cage, she was coming around to us. She really took to us, especially me, while in Nicholas's room. Like Patches, she would come to me quickly, usually plopping on top of me, and begin to purr. She loved and still loves to "cruise" around us. If I was sitting on the

floor leaning with my back against the wall, she would make circles around me, making sure to slip behind and through my legs before settling down. She would curl up into a ball, usually on my upper thighs, and look up at me and purr.

Apricot, simply put, has a wonderful personality. He's a lover, not a fighter. He loves everyone, and usually gets vocal when wrestling with his brothers and sister. I know when they're picking on him. He's the one crying out. In Nicholas's room when I was sitting on the floor, he would settle on my ankles. Always. Like Patches and Sabrina, he wanted to be in physical contact with me. There were many nights when we would go up to bed with Nicholas and sit on the floor, covered with kittens, all except for Mickey.

Mickey would always sit near me, purring very loudly, but always just outside of easy arm's reach. I was worried about him; was he

anti-social? Would he get more aloof? I believe that he simply doesn't like physical contact with us. He sits nearby and purrs while looking at me. But try to reach over to grab him, and he's gone, like a puff of air. He'll tolerate it when I grab him, and he's always circling our feet, especially during feeding time. And, he'll look me in the eye and meow with his high-pitched voice. When I'm successful in pulling him up, he purrs like crazy. I can just tell he's not comfortable. But he's very cute, especially his face, a bright pink nose surrounded by white fur, similar to what a white bunny might be like.

This therapy was probably what got us mentally through the darkest time for our family. We had to borrow money from friends and family to simply pay the mortgage and for food. Believing that there's no end to the tunnel, or worse, that the light at the end of the tunnel is an oncoming train, and that we're trapped is an incredibly awful feeling. And as the family provider, having the family that depends on me going down the drain beside me, made it that much worse. I think that's why the kittens have such a special place in our hearts. We all came through that time as a new combined stronger family. That's a hard concept for some of our extended human family to understand. These kittens are our family, as are our two older cats. We could not give them up, just like we couldn't give up our own children.

This perplexes some of our extended family. They simply don't understand our choice, and probably never will. My sisters, who take after my mom, are animal lovers. They get us. My mom grew up in Iran in the 1930's with a menagerie of animals pretty much every animal imaginable. I guess that apple didn't fall far from the tree; my wife's side not so much.

Finally, it came time to have the kittens spayed and neutered. We grabbed the kittens, placed them into a carrier, and drove off to the vet. As we were officially fostering the kittens, this was arranged through the humane society. Nicholas and I dropped them off at the vet in the morning and worried for the rest of the day until it was time to pick them up. I went back to the vet to pick them up before they closed. The boys were fine without complications. As fine as they could be losing their manhood, that is. The only lasting effect seems to be Mickey's high-pitched meow. We call it "squirrelly." Poor Mickey; he's the biggest of the kittens, but has the tiniest meow.

Sabrina, however, had some internal bleeding, and had to be re-anesthetized, reopened, and re-stitched. She had to stay the night; more worry. Monica and I waited anxiously for news of Sabrina. I paced the entire day. Monica called from work several times to see if I had any news. Was Sabrina all right? Imagine the worry we had for this little darling, after just a few months of having her! Today, she's sitting next to me, purring, as I write this.

Finally it came time to pick her up. The drive to the vet was excruciating. She had recovered from the second surgery with no more internal bleeding. We had a relaxing drive home from the vet. It was great to have Sabrina rejoin the family. The kittens were glad to see their sister. So now they were back and starting to return to their normal selves. We kept an eye on Sabrina's stitches and were careful when picking her up. She seemed none the worse for the wear, climbing, exploring, and playing with her brothers.

Toward the end of February 2010 we were finally able to access my pension and begin withdrawing from it. This gave us much-needed funds and a return to a somewhat normal life. This allowed us to pay our bills and mortgage again. And I was finally starting to see some nibbles in the job market; this, after over a year of drought!

Spring was soon in full bloom. It's my favorite time of the year. Everything greens up, the weather gets warmer, the kittens are happy, and our family is stable. Kittens sitting in sunshine on the windowsill; it does not get any better than this.

It's March 2010, crunch time. It was also time to officially adopt them. Once we had funds, it was easy to make the adoption legal. Do we adopt the kittens or give them away? Adoption is such a simple idea. Thankfully, the Flower Mound Humane Society made it so easy. I met with the Humane Society folks at the local PetSmart, where they were showing pets for adoption, and presto, they were Zekulins! We simply formalized the decision that was made months earlier. And now, there were six!

The kittens were spending more time out of Nicholas's room. The family playroom connects Nicholas's bedroom with the bathroom upstairs. This is where the big cats' litter box sits. Obviously, with the kittens out in the playroom exploring, they would check out the litter box. So, off I go to PetSmart to upgrade the litter box. Apparently, the rule of thumb is one litter box per cat, plus one, in the house. I wasn't aware of this veterinary guideline. We have the most wonderful vets at the Valley Ranch Pet Clinic, (in Valley Ranch, TX) Dr. Greg Rouchon and Dr. Tina Capps. And their staff is wonderful too!

The playroom was a mess. It really was more of a storage room, with a TV in it. For the kittens, it was a new place to explore. They excelled at testing gravity and its uses in entertainment. Patches and Sabrina were starting to develop their sense of balance, especially on the display shelves. They could jump up on the shelves and even jump up from shelf to shelf. Needless to say, some "important" toys and collectables were gravity tested, and subsequently stored away to some place "safer."

With the kittens at play, we had to make sure that we eliminated obvious hazards, like string, rope, cord, small edible toy parts, plastic bags, sharp objects, heavy objects that could fall, collectibles that could break, collectibles that already broke, etc. Plus, we would put things away that the cats found that we thought they could hurt themselves with. They didn't hurt themselves; they just ran around in the two rooms and were kittens. We did have a recliner chair that the kittens loved to hide under, especially when we were trying to get them back into Nicholas's room. Occasionally they wouldn't come out from under the recliner, and we'd have to extract them. This was particularly true for Mickey, who was becoming even more afraid of our touch.

As the other kittens were more accepting of our touch and allowed us to pretty much do anything with them, Mickey would still stay just beyond arm's length. He would always stay near us and played with his brothers and sisters, but when one of us got into the mix, he would sit just beyond arm's length. In the words of Bugs Bunny, this means war. The more he stayed away from us, the more we tried to hold him, figuring that what he lacked was our soothing love. After all, it worked on the other three kittens.

Mickey is a warm loving kitten, just not to us humans. He has a funny quirk. He loves to butt heads with the other cats. This can lead to some funny situations. As I'm opening cat food and the cats gather, I hear a thud. Two heads, usually its Mickey and Apricot, butting heads. It sounds painful, but since they continue to do it, it must not hurt. Mickey head butts all of the other cats, too. His brothers and sister don't mind, and actually kind of like it. But Koko and Tigger are another matter.

One of he funniest things I've seen the kittens do is when Mickey comes up *behind* Koko and head butts him, from the side. Koko's reaction is one of surprise, shock, and disgust. He jumps, meows, and tries to swat Mickey, who just ignores him and keeps on going. It's kind of like a drive-by head bumping. Also, Mickey can be spotted curled up with his brothers or sister on a cat bed. It's cute to see.

_3_ Freedom!

Springtime! It was April in North Texas, the best time of the year. The trees are quickly greening up, the pear trees are blooming, and after fifteen months of being unemployed, I finally landed a job. It was a software sales job; build a sales pipeline, as fast as possible. All the work at half the salary! I'm not complaining. We had benefits! Now we could withdraw less from my pension to make ends meet. It was a start in the right direction. But most of all, I had purpose and finally, some hope.

The time came to move the kittens out of Nicholas's room and give them free reign in the house. Although they each had escaped from the playroom into the house, and been brought back, with lots of screaming and chasing, it was time to simply open the door and let them run in the house. At first, they ran out like they would while escaping, but then stopped to see what we were doing. They would look back to see if we were chasing them; then, they were off. Now they had each been to various parts of the house and interacted with each of our two older cats and us. But that was under our supervision. Here, we moved the litter box, food bowls, and scratching post into the rest of the house. Although they would come up to Nicholas's room and visit, they didn't stay there long.

Sometimes, during the first couple of nights they would be up in Nicholas's room with us. But overall the kittens preferred to stay in other parts of the house. This was great for Tigger, who reclaimed Nicholas's bedroom the first night. Tigger went back to sleeping with Nicholas, wrapping himself around his head on Nicholas's pillow. There was many a morning that I would find Tigger sleeping squarely on Nicholas's pillow, and Nicholas would be scrunched down, off the pillow.

Now that the kittens were free to roam about the house, they could discover new places to hide, sleep, sun, and overall make their own. At first, their favorite sleeping spot became under our bed, then on our bed, then anywhere in our bedroom. Of course, we got a couple of little cat beds for them. We placed them strategically on our bed so as to have cats sleeping near us, and not necessarily on us. Another favorite place to hang was the kitchen, which provided both entertainment (fish tank) and close proximity to food. The morning sunshine, thanks to all of the windows, and kitchen table and chair provided perfect sunning spots. The kitchen provided one more thing; exercise, specifically climbing and jumping up on our counter, fridge, and cabinets, the higher the better. At first, the kittens could just jump to the counter. This was inconvenient, but manageable. As they have grown the kittens' climbing and jumping abilities improved greatly to the point that nothing was impossible, or at least the kittens thought so.

It became necessary to move breakables that were in the way of a downward kitten. It wasn't uncommon to hear a crash of some sort during the night. We were worried about broken glass, etc. We began moving anything breakable out of the way. Apricot was the first to climb onto the kitchen cabinets by leaping from the countertop. If his front paws made it, he would pull himself up using his leg (with claws) strength. Shortly thereafter, Patches demonstrated that he could do it, then had to one-up Apricot by jumping across from one cabinet to another, about four feet away, and eight feet up in the air! Soon Sabrina had to show she was as good as the boys. The only one who's not a big climber is Mickey. At first he was content to stay on the ground, or close to it, but now, he climbs like to rest of them.

Another room that became a favorite was our home office. The room faces south. The windows are a perfect solarium. Even today, cats and kittens alike can be seen sunning themselves on the windowsills. The office, with the computers and sunshine, is usually the warmest room in the house, a natural resting place for cats, especially in the winter. And since I spend a good part of my day here as well, I get to see them interact here as well.

There are a lot of wires and cables in the office, so I have to make sure there's nothing overly dangerous here. My office is messy, so I really have to make sure that all wires and cables aren't a cat noose waiting to happen, especially when we're not around the house.

Sabrina, as it turns out, has an interesting habit of chewing cables. I found this out when my mouse stopped working. I found it disconnected from the cable. It's now a wireless wired mouse! I just hope she doesn't chew on a power cable. In addition to Sabrina chewing cables, the office has to contend with Tigger chewing paper, so it's important not to leave important papers out. Mickey likes to sit on top of stuff on the floor, making an impromptu nest. And, of course, all of the cats take turns sunning themselves.

Koko has a bed in there, which on rare occasions gets occupied by another cat, but it's amazing how they avoid his bed. They'll walk, jump, and leap all around it, but generally avoid bothering him when he's in the bed. And this room isn't immune to the kittens' climbing. Apricot, Tigger, and sometimes Mickey and Sabrina all take turns climbing on shelves, and desks. And of course, the cats have to make sure that gravity still works, so they will send something to the ground, usually as a reminder to us about being messy.

And of course, the new favorite room is our bathroom. This is the ultimate cat gathering spot, as they wait for me to start my day and feed them. During the night there are a number of cat driven activities that usually result in a sound that wakes me up. These activities include, but are not limited to, cat chasing through the bathroom, in and out of the tub, climbing on (and occasionally into the hamper, on top of the shower stall wall, clothes sorting, and, of course, gravity testing.

I get to watch this as I'm getting ready for the day. I can be combing my hair or shaving when a cat will fly through, followed closely by another in hot pursuit, usually followed by a scream and a growl. Apricot loves heights, so he's the first to climb the shower wall. We have a shower with tiles on top of the wall that gives a nice perch to look down on everyone. Occasionally, Patches or Sabrina joins Apricot. All it takes is a noise to get them to jump down. They're especially afraid of the hair dryer.

As I mentioned, the cats all like to gather around me while I'm getting ready for the day. Usually, this means one of the cats will sit in the room, in a position where he or she can observe my actions. And if it looks like I'm done, he or she can alert the others that breakfast is on its way. During the morning, the kittens are the first to wake and track me, although Koko is usually in a prime location overseeing things. As the kittens have gotten older, they seem to be more of a pain to Koko and Tigger. Koko usually sits in the main doorway and swats at kittens as they run by. I can tell when a kitten runs by on its way to the bathroom, as there's a certain meow that Koko uses as he swats at a kitten. Koko uses the same meow and also swats at Tigger as he passes by as well. Go figure. We just call Koko the grumpus among us.

The kittens gather, usually with the first to keep an eye on me, followed by successive arrivals, which then strategically lay down to observe my actions. One of the most interesting behaviors is Patches' obsession with the water in the shower, after we're done with the shower. Before the door is opened he gathers near it. And, as I step out Patches is in the shower, passing my feet to get in. He sits and waits for the showerhead to clear and drop some water, which he tries to catch with his paws.

Sometimes another kitten will come with him, but soon leaves out of boredom. But Patches will sit, sometimes for fifteen to twenty minutes. When he comes out he's usually pretty wet, especially his paws and tail. He likes nothing more than stopping by to sit on me, and dry himself. Ah, the joys of a cold wet kitty on my warm dry self. Other times he'll be running around or climbing on furniture and slips off or slides on the tile with his wet paws. It's pretty funny. It kind of makes up for the cold, wet paws on my nice warm dry self. There's been many a morning where I can see a wet paw print on the tile floor.

This brings me to an interesting phenomenon that adopting a whole litter allows us to see and observe; kitten and cat family dynamics. Having a whole litter is very different than adopting a single cat, or even two unrelated cats (as we had previously done), especially if the litter is tightly bonded, as ours is. Although they're unique individuals, they also have their common bond, which we get to see play out every day. While they can sleep together on our bed, usually they sleep as individuals, near each other but not usually touching.

Sometimes Patches and Sabrina might sleep on one another, but not that often. In the morning, when I shuffle out of bed, a designated watch cat accompanies me; a designated kitten that sits nearby, observing my actions, making sure I'm moving toward their morning goal; food. Sometimes I could swear they communicate telepathically. The minute the cat observes my progress in the bathroom, the others begin showing up there.

Sometimes, the horde arrives together, sometimes individually. Usually, they follow each other in. The first arrives, followed by a succession of three kittens. Usually the first sits down and observes while the others arrive. As I mentioned before, Koko's meow can accompany the kittens' arrivals as they dodge his swipes. Usually Patches would arrive first. He would sit someplace where he could observe me and anything else he wanted to keep an eye on; next, either Sabrina or Apricot, depending on who would brave Koko first. They would assume other strategic positions or begin to explore some part of the bathroom that interested them. Sabrina loves to sit *in* the bathtub. From there, she can sit and see absolutely nothing, but she still likes it. Apricot would go for the high ground. Mickey would jump past Koko and arrive just in time for me to start walking in the direction he just came from, and he would turn around, jump past Koko, again, who would swipe and meow a second time.

I mentioned clothes sorting earlier. At times, when the hamper is overflowing and clothes happen to be left on the floor, it can provide entertainment for the kittens. When the tile is cold, the clothes provide a spot to keep the paws warm. At other times, I come into the bathroom and the clothes have been strewn about the whole bathroom. The first few times this happened, Monica and I accused each other of leaving a mess. Eventually, we figured out that the kittens simply loved to play with the clothes pile, much like we did as kids with leaf piles we had raked up in the fall. And, as these sharply clawed kittens flew through the clothes pile, they would catch a shirt or sock and it would fly by.

The kittens were both fascinated and scared of the toilets. Sabrina would run away upon hearing the flush, but then run back and stand on her two hind legs, bracing her front paws on the side of the bowl, and looking at the swirling water. I'm so glad that's all she did.

Now, connecting to our bathroom is our closet. Let's just say it's full. And let's just say that there are lots of places where a kitten could go and hide, and a kitten wouldn't be easily found, unless that kitten wanted to be found. As I mentioned earlier, Apricot has this talent of opening doors. And our closet doors (French doors) are his favorite, after the bathroom doors (also French doors). He's good. And as he's gotten older, he's very good. In fact, he's the doorsmith! So it's not uncommon to find the bathroom and closet doors open after being out of the house. And, of course, the party is in the closet. The kittens were good at climbing, and when surprising them, it wasn't uncommon to see them scatter from different levels of the closet shelves, behind clothes that were hanging.

A couple of times, the kittens have gotten into things they shouldn't have. The kittens have found my wife's fur slippers that I gave her as a gift that she never wears. She had them put away high on a shelf in our closet. For some reason these slippers fascinate the kittens. I've had to take them away a couple of times. It wasn't unheard of to close the closet doors with a kitten inside. Sabrina or Apricot and sometimes Mickey are the usual suspects.

Once Sabrina spent a whole day in there. We closed the closet doors after making sure there were no kittens in there. We didn't notice she was missing until dinner, and she wasn't there. We heard a faint meow and scratching coming from our closet. We flung open the doors, and out she comes, happy to be free. What finally got the kittens' evicted from the closet were some freshly scratched new shoes. After that, we're careful to keep them out, most of the time.

Feeding time; the most important time for a kitten to be present and show the food bearer how much they love him/her. As we would start to work in the kitchen before a meal, cats and kittens would take notice and begin to arrive. Koko was always first. Since he's with us around the house, he's there when the action starts. Patches is usually the first kitten to arrive, followed by Sabrina, then Mickey. Appy is usually last. This is especially true in the evening, when he's likely to be sleeping. Talk about a sleepy looking face!

In the morning he's usually there with the rest of them. This is when Koko's head butting may occur. It's always worth a good laugh. As I start pouring the dry food, I can hear purring and feel cats and kittens circulating behind my legs. It's not uncommon to turn around and be staring right at Patches, who loves to sit on the island counter across from the sink where I prepare the cats' meals. Sometimes Sabrina will join him. Apricot will meow and paw at the cabinet door, trying to open it. He can open cabinets, too!

He also has an interesting habit of giving me "love nibbles". As I'm preparing their food, the cats circulate around my feet. Appy will stop and nibble on my calf. The nibble is something like I would do while eating corn on the cob, small quick bites. It hurts and tickles at the same time. I really hope he is not checking tenderness of my calves.

Finally, when I'm ready to feed them, I'll grab their bowls and head over to their feeding spot. First, I feed Koko, then the rest, and last Tigger, who's usually by himself. As I'm carrying their bowls, the kittens move between my feet, weaving in and out. It's like standing in a stream ankle-deep as the water passes through your feet. This is the Flow of Kittens! Nicholas thought of this name as we both discovered this phenomenon. At first, we told each other about the kittens weaving between our legs, and after Nicholas coined the phrase, I knew that I had the title of this book.

Momma is still out there almost every day and evening. Sometimes we see her slinking through the grass in the yard or climbing the fence or even sunning herself on the porch. The kittens have all seen her eating on the porch. I usually feed her right after I feed the kittens. Usually one or two of them will watch her eat just like Koko and Tigger watched them eat. Sometimes there might be another cat waiting his turn to eat after Momma. We figure that one of those cats is Daddy cat; may even be both of them! One of the wildest things we've seen Momma do is to jump up onto the outside ledge of our bathroom window and sit.

The interesting part is that this window is a good eight feet up in the air. She gets up to it by jumping of on the back yard fence. And most of the time that we've seen her up there was to sun herself and also to keep out of the rain. That window has a brick ledge wide enough for her to sit on. It's high and safe. Plus, she gets a good view of the surrounding yards. Now I know where the kittens get their love of heights. Well, most cats seem to like heights, but not all. Koko prefers to stay on the ground.

Patches has a lot to tell. He has this wonderful look about him as he sits on me looking straight into my eyes. I do believe he's smiling. Both he and Sabrina have been my muses, my inspiration to write. It's funny how quickly life can change, for better or worse, but I'm a glass-is-half-full kind of person. The best is yet to come!

Patches is quite a character. When he sees me after having slept or been in another part of the house, he starts following me around like a puppy. As I walk around the house, he runs next to me, jumping from the floor to the end-tables right as I pass them, then to the countertop and back to the floor. As he's been doing this for some time, he now will run slightly in front of me anticipating my moves and paths around the house. He'll start in the kitchen and run to the bedroom, then to the bathroom. He'll bounce on the bathroom vanity and stare at me. Sometimes I fake him out by going to the home office, which is a right instead of a left to the bedroom.

However, by the time I get to the office, he's right next to me. Finally, when I stop and sit down he's on me and settles down into my arms, with a purr right into my ears. When it comes to stress relief, Patches is the best! As I sit here writing, I can feel my blood pressure drop, my heart rate slowing down, and calm taking over. My worries disappear, my mind focuses as my ears send soothing signals to my brain. The gentle purr of a happy kitten has its intended effect on me. It's a great way to end a busy day!

Patches' Tail

4 My first memory, Momma

I'm warm. I'm content. My stomach is full. I feel comfortable. I see my sister sleeping nearby. The sun is shining on the big soft couch. My sister is awake. I'll watch her. Maybe I'll stalk her! Wait, she's watching something. She's getting ready to pounce! One of our brothers is walking past us. She's stalking him! She pounces; he's startled. Figures, he's not that observant. They wrestle; he runs off, she chases him. They move off and sit in the sunshine. I'm falling asleep. I'm warm. My belly is full. The man below me moves. I have to make sure he doesn't push me off. Good, he stopped moving. I can go back to sleep. The man is nice and warm, big, too. There's a lot of room to sleep on.

It's nice inside this big house, warm in spots, cool in others. There's lots of food, and the people are nice. My brothers and sister are safe. We're together, except Momma. She's outside. Here, there are no dogs to chase us; no loud machines that come by and scare us. I remember what it was like to be hiding outside from the people, the scary animals that chased us, and the dark cave that smelled awful. But playing out in the sun with my brothers and sister was fun.

It was a while ago, now. Life outside of the house was scary, but was also exciting. We had lots of places to play and hide. We followed Momma and she showed us how to pounce and how to catch things to eat, what not to eat; things that would make you sick. She taught us how to stay hidden in the bushes behind things, how to lie out in the sun and soak it up.

My first memory is of Momma. She was warm and had a nice purr that made me feel safe. I remember drinking milk and feeling all warm inside, pushing my paws against her belly. My brothers and sister were next to me, all cuddled up, keeping warm in the dark smelly cave. I remember hearing strange noises over our heads. It was a rumbling, like a distant thunder, that would start slowly coming from one direction, get louder, and scarier, then it would pass over our heads and move away in the other direction. Momma would quiet us and tell us we were safe, that the noise wouldn't hurt us down here. Sometimes other cats and even other strange animals would come down into the cave, and Momma would stand between us and the other cat and let out a warning growl and hiss. Most of the times the other cats would leave, but sometimes they would come nearer, and Momma would let out the fiercest growl, then hiss so loudly.

One time, a strange animal came down into our cave, and started moving toward us. Momma let out a warning growl, but that animal didn't stop. It had scary red eyes that were glued on Momma. It came closer, and Momma let loose the loudest scariest growl I had ever heard. The red-eyed beast kept coming closer. Finally, Momma sprang on it so fast that even the beast was startled. Momma attacked it, biting and clawing at it. It looked like there were two or three Mommas attacking it.

The fight was short. The beast ran away yelping. Momma stood there making sure it was gone, up and out of the cave, back to the outside where it had come from. My brothers and sister were also scared, but we were mesmerized, watching Momma protect us and to see what happened. Momma told us to always be weary of other animals, both the four-legged kind and the two-legged kind, the people above us. Momma said that they had chased her many times, but they were too slow.

The cave was cool compared to the air outside. It was dark and smelly, but sometimes the wind would blow and we could smell the grass and trees from above. The air from outside was hot in the daytime and cooler at night. In the morning, we could smell the grass. It's a magical smell, before all of the noises and people and animals ruin things.

Momma would go out to catch things to eat in the evenings and warn us to stay and not move. It was scary when the noises would come above us, and Momma wasn't there to make us feel safe. The four of us would huddle together for protection and make us feel safer. Sometimes she would be gone for a long time. It was great when we heard her chirp to us. We knew she was back and all was well. As we grew a little older, when she was gone, we would walk around and explore the cave. It smelled bad, and sometimes we would see water and even snakes down below. Later, when we were older, Momma taught us how to catch the little snakes. She warned us about some snakes that could kill a cat.

One time, there was a strong and long rain outside, and the cave was surrounded by fast flowing water. I could see Momma was worried that the water might come up to where we were in the cave. I think that was the scariest moment of my life. But Momma kept us calm, warm, and dry. Her purr was reassuring. She picked a good spot in the cave for us to live. We could see things moving in the fast water, sticks, and grass, and even other things I had never seen before.

The rain stopped, and later the water stopped flowing into the cave. Momma drank some of the water and called us to drink. It was cool and tasted good. We could see lots of new things on the bottom of the cave that weren't there before the rain; new rocks, mud, and even a dead snake!

From where we slept in the cave, I could see light from outside. That's where a lot of the noise we heard would come from; strange noises, dogs barking and walking overhead, other animals yelling, running. And we heard the two-legged people outside. Every once in a while we'd hear the people make load and scary noises with machines that would move along the grass above us, making shaking noises that we could feel. Those people would leave as quickly as they came, and all would be quiet again.

Sometimes, the smaller people who were running and yelling outside would start to yell louder. I could hear them running toward our cave entrance, more yelling, then something round would fall into our cave, bounce around, and stop. I was curious about that round thing, but Momma would tell us to sit still and be quiet until the little people went away from our cave. One time, when they left, I ran down to see what it was. It had stopped moving. I've never seen nor smelled anything like it before. It was a bright yellow, fuzzy, round rock that smelled awful. I tapped it. It moved around and stopped. I tapped it again, harder. It moved farther and rolled down the cave and bounced as it rolled. The little people above us were playing with bouncy, moldy rocks. Very weird!

One day, when we could climb out of the cave, Momma told us to follow her. It was time to see what was outside of the cave. My sister was as excited as I was, but my two brothers were worried and maybe a little scared. I know I was. It was getting darker, and not so hot outside. Momma jumped up and out of the cave, as I've seen her do many times before. She chirped that it was safe, and I followed her.

The sun shined right on me. It felt so warm! I looked around. I was standing on a big flat white rock that was still warm from the sun. There was a lot of grass and big trees, and lots of big strange things that looked like big rocks all lined up next to the big warm white rock. I stuck my nose up and smelled the air. I could smell many things; the grass, the trees, and other things that I had never smelled before. They smelled wonderful, especially compared to the cave. Momma chirped to me to follow her. My brothers and sister jumped out next to me looked around, and smelled the air, just as I did, then we all ran after Momma.

We followed Momma to some big trees, then to some bushes near one of those big rocks. Momma said these were where the two-legged people lived. And people made those scary loud noises we heard in the cave. They went inside those big metal things that rolled on the ground just like the smelly moldy yellow rock I saw in our cave. Those big metal things made noise and smelled bad, and that's what the two-legged people did. Momma said they did walk and run around a lot, too.

The bushes were all along the bottom of the big stone rock, and we ran underneath them and gathered together. Momma told us that now that we were out of the cave, we were always in danger, and had to watch out all of the time. She said that danger could come from anywhere, and that most of the time these bushes were a great place to hide. She told us that there were lots of different animals out here, some of which came to our cave at night. These animals could hurt us and kill us! There were flying animals that could swoop down from the sky and grab us, and we would disappear forever! There were lots of dogs in this area, and most of them would bark at us and chase us, but the people whom they were with would keep them from chasing us too much. The dogs liked to walk with the people when the sun was low in the sky.

She also told us about what we could eat out here. There were lots of little animals we could catch and eat, and that this is what she would do at night. She taught us to play games that would help us learn how to hunt those animals. Momma told us to stay away from the tree in front of one of these houses, because that's where the mother rabbit and her babies lived, and that Momma went by too close one time, and the mother rabbit attacked her, just like Momma did to that red-eyed beast. From that point on, Momma has stayed away from the tree and the rabbit.

One thing we soon discovered was that those big square stony rocks was where the people lived. The sun warmed those people's homes. The stones near them were nice to lie on and stayed warm even after the sun went down. We didn't go too far from our cave, and Momma always went in first, to make sure that there were no beasts waiting for us in the cave.

On other days, we'd go out by the people's home and sit in the bushes in front or lie out on the stones to sun ourselves. One of the people's homes was our favorite. It was near the cave and had lots of bushes, and sometimes we'd see other cats inside that home. They would see us walk by, and they would run around and look at us. But we couldn't hear nor smell them, but we could see them. They could see us, and my brother and sister would laugh and roll around in front of them to tease them. They would run around and look at us.

My sister walked right in front of them stuck her tail high in the air, and just strolled right in front of a gray cat! I could see him react! It was fun. We'd come out and do that on many nights. The big rock had a nice stony place behind the bushes. Here we were safe from the animals in front, and it was bright as daytime there, even when it was nighttime. We could hide in the bushes if something scared us.

One day we were playing outside in the bushes by our favorite house. We were running around, hiding, and practicing pouncing on one another. Momma would show us how to lie still in wait, until just the right moment then pounce. I remember that Momma is a great hunter. I was practicing my pounce on my sister. She was walking by when I jumped on her. She was surprised, but grabbed onto me, and we rolled on the ground, behind the bushes. Then one of my brothers pounced on me, and I grabbed him, and we rolled out of the bushes and onto a long, hard, flat stone in front of the house where the people lived. Suddenly, we saw them and froze. The little people were out in front of the house. It looked like they were playing, too! My brother and I quickly ran back into the bushes. Whew, they didn't see us. Our hearts were racing; it was fun, hiding from those people and watching them from the bushes. Then my sister pounced on me!

We slept well that night, all curled up in the bushes. It was warm outside, and the setting sun felt good on us and made us sleepy. The next morning I was awakened by the sound of a dog sniffing by the bushes. My brothers and sisters were now awake, too. I could tell they were scared. Momma wasn't with us. We were alone. I would defend us from that dog. I moved up front to face it. But then I heard one of the people calling at the dog and pulling on a rope attached to its neck. The dog decided to run back to its master. I showed that dog that I was the master of these bushes! Then my sister pounced on me, and we rolled around in the bushes. Momma came back later. She had brought some food that she had caught. We all ate it. We told her about the dog sniffing in the bushes.

Momma warned us to be careful. A dog could easily sneak up on us, especially here behind the bushes. Momma would let us sleep on the stone, but kept a watchful eye on the entrance to the flat stone, and would warn us if something were coming. A few times we would run and hide in the bushes. We'd walk around to other houses and hide in those bushes, running between houses or climbing a fence, like Momma showed us. She was fast!

One day, later in the day, when the sun was getting ready to set, we were sleeping in the bushes by the house with the little people. I could hear the little people yelling, running, and playing. Then they were quiet. I peeked out of the bushes and could see they had stopped running and pouncing, and were sitting near the grass, not far from the entrance to our cave. They were talking and laughing. I moved back into the bushes to see what my brothers and sister were doing. My brothers were sleeping. Then my sister pounced on me. I yelped and ran away. She chased me. My brothers awoke and started chasing me. Then I chased them. Suddenly, we all froze. The little people were looking at us.

They yelled in excitement and ran toward us. "Hide!" I told my sister. "Hide in the bushes." I told my brothers. We ran into the bushes.

The little people were now looking in the bushes, trying to find us. We hid behind the biggest bush and huddled together. They would never find us. Soon, they ran to their homes. One of the little people ran into the home by the bushes we were hiding in. He called out to the other people to come out to see what he had found. Suddenly there were more people outside looking for us in the bushes. We huddled even tighter together behind the biggest branches we could find. When they couldn't see us, they gave up and left.

Later, when no one was around, we relaxed and moved around in the bushes. Momma came back and brought us some food. After that, we played on the flat stone place in front of the house, but behind the bushes. In addition to seeing cats watching us, we could see the people in the house. They were watching us, too. We played and rolled around. My sister pounced on me, and I pounced on her. And we rolled around some more. The people were still watching us.

The next day, we were playing on the big flat stone behind the bushes again. The people and cats were there, watching us again. Part of the stone was in the sun, and was warm. It was nice to feel the sun, and the warmth of the stone; perfect to sleep on!

Suddenly there was a noise from the big stone house. A part of it opened and a man stepped out. We ran like our lives depended on it, straight into the bushes. We watched, our hearts racing with fear. He bent down and put something on the ground, then looked in our direction. Our hearts leapt. Then he went back into his house. I could see him by the window, looking at what he put down. I could smell something interesting in the air. It was coming from what he put down. Momma told us to stay in the bushes. She went to investigate what the man put down. I could see Momma going near the thing the man had put down, smelling it. Then she was eating as fast as she could. We all ran to see what smelled so interesting and what she was eating. It was food!

As I think back to that moment, I realize that having food "given" to you is pretty nice. It beats trying to hunt for it or find it somewhere. There were a lot of times we stayed hungry because we couldn't find something to eat. I do miss hunting sometimes. Hunting also reminds me of Momma, teaching us how to stalk, hide, and pounce. That's why

I like to stalk my brothers and sister, and even the other two cats in the house. It's fun, and I like to see the look of surprise on their faces, although they like to stalk me, too.

Now, back to the story. We ate the food along with Momma. It was different than a live kill, but tastier than things like bugs or worms. It did smell pretty good. The man had put enough of it out so that we were all full, even Momma. She licked the food from the strange thing it was in and even ate what we left on the ground. The sun was still warming the stone. It felt warm, and suddenly I was sleepy. We all were. Momma lay down near the bushes and kept watch as my brothers and I slept. I'm not sure where my sister went. I fell asleep before I could see where she went. A little while later I awoke. The sun was going down, but the stone was still warm. Momma called us to go back into hiding. I could see the people still watching us.

The next day, Momma was showing us more tricks to hunt better, but we heard the man come out and put down more food. We ran to the food and started eating. Momma ate, but then kept an eye out on the people who were still watching us eat. He came out later that day with more food. Each time, the food was different. I hadn't smelled anything like it before! This time it was really good. The food had a tasty liquid in it. It made the meat taste better. When we were really hungry, we would eat all of the food and lick the liquid till it was all gone. After that, I'd make sure to lick my face and paws clean. It was nice to sit in the sun and lick myself clean. And, of course, I was done first and would then pounce on my sister.

It was nice to have a full belly and sleep in the sun. On some days, it would rain. The bushes kept us dry most of the time. Sometimes it would rain hard, and even the ground under the bushes would get wet, and the rain would drip on us. It was fun to catch the raindrops from the bushes. Sometimes I would catch the rain in my mouth and other times with my paw. I was getting pretty good at catching the rain. My brothers and sister didn't seem too interested in catching the rain; they were more interested in staying dry. It's okay. I was the best hunter and catcher of all of us, except Momma, of course. She was proud of my hunting skills and would praise me and give me encouragement.

Sometimes, when we were sleeping, I'd wake up and see Momma going away to find food. I decided to follow her. I ran off behind her. She knew I was behind her, but this time she let me follow. She said she was going to try to catch a flying animal in a tree and bring that for us to eat. We climbed a tall wooden wall that stretched between two different people's homes. We climbed it. Momma jumped and was at the top in a blink of an eye. I jumped, but had to climb and climb, but I couldn't get to the top, and let go. I dropped to the ground and let out a yell to Momma. Momma told me to slip through the hole in the wall, next to one of the houses. She was so smart. I slipped through and could see Momma dropping down near me. Then she bristled and let out a meow; a warning! I slid back near the hole in the wall. Momma let out another meow and a hiss, this one louder and angrier. Suddenly I could see what Momma was looking at.

It was another cat! It wasn't Dad cat. This was another cat, and Momma was madder than I had seen her in a while. Her fur was up, her fangs were out, and she was ready to attack. I was scared, but still watched in fascination. Momma was protecting me. The other cat was big, and he was looking at Momma, but didn't seem worried. Then he saw me, and that's when Momma attacked him. Momma pounced on him so fast, even I couldn't believe how fast she flew. She let out a meow and scream like I've never heard from her, except that one time under the ground. It was over as fast as it started. The other cat ran away so fast and so far. Momma chased him for a moment, but then turned quickly toward me, to make sure I was safe. That's my Momma! She was tender to us, and ferocious to anyone who wanted to hurt us!

That's the first time I went hunting with Momma. I went exploring with her every day. We'd go to see what was going on in our patch. We went over and around the wooden walls, and even climbed trees. We hid in bushes when scary things came our way. Every few days, Momma would gather us and take us to another safe place. That was when the noisy people would come and make the grass smell so nice. They came in a loud smelly rolling thing and made loud scary vibrations. We would run when they were coming. They would walk over the grass and make strange loud noises that hurt our ears. One time, we didn't run as far away as usual, and hid deep in the bushes by the wooden wall and watched the people make noise. They made the grass smell fresh, like when I chewed it. The whole grassy area smelled like that. That's it; they came to chew the grass! And then they made even more noise and made the grass blow like the wind. It was strange. Then, as quickly as they came, they left, sometimes going to other grassy areas nearby. Finally, when they left, it would be peaceful and calm; we could come out of hiding. All of the grass had been chewed and smelled strong. The wind would blow that smell away, but I could still taste that smell, especially when we walked on the freshly chewed grass. After walking on it, we would stop and clean our paws, licking off the grass juice. It was pretty tasty. Momma said this was good for us.

Another time, Momma took all of us hunting. It was still hot, and we weren't used to staying together very well. Momma did her best to keep us together. She would call to us to hurry and stay in the shadows. She warned of birds that would swoop down and carry a kitten away. When we were following Momma, we'd practice pouncing on each other. If one of us got separated, Momma would call out, and we'd call back. Momma would then run back and push us along. If we were too slow, she would grab us and carry us. That was fun! Sometimes we'd play slowpoke, to see how long it would take for Momma to come and carry us.

One time, as we were running between trees, Momma called to us, but in a way that meant she wasn't playing around. She called, but one of my brothers was looking at a worm on the ground. Suddenly, Momma's ears shot out, then down, and she ran like the wind toward him. I had never seen her run so fast! Then we heard a strange call from above. It was one of those birds, and it was swooping down toward my brother. Momma screamed at him. He started to run, but froze. He scrunched down as low as he could go. Then I saw a shadow from the bird over my brother. And just as the bird came into view, Momma jumped into the air toward the swooping bird. The bird suddenly saw Momma and was distracted. It landed for a blink of an eye, then was gone back into the air. At first, I thought that the bird had hit Momma. It all happened so fast. Momma scooped up my brother and ran with him toward the bushes we were all now hiding in.

When she got to us, she dropped him and turned toward the daylight, watching to make sure the bird was gone. Our hearts were beating so fast and so loud. My brother's was beating even faster. When Momma was sure it was safe, she turned to us and scolded us, and told us of the danger of being out in the open, especially during the day. She said even at night, we had to be careful; there were birds that hunted kittens at night!

I didn't sleep well that night. I kept seeing birds swooping down into our home in the cave under the big hot stone and carrying us away as we screamed for Momma. I would wake up, and feel my brothers and sister next to me. Momma was curled up next to us, keeping us warm. It was starting to get cool at night.

I remember Momma playing with us. There were times we would all jump on her and try to pounce on her. That was fun to do, especially if she was sleeping. We'd all be sleeping, but I would wake up and start sneaking toward her. Then, I would pounce, landing on her belly. She'd get startled, then relax, when she saw it was me. We had a lot of fun, rolling around on Momma. When we started to grow up, we would pounce and practice pinning our pray with our paws, then going in for the kill.

Momma's ears were fun to grab, as she would be moving them to keep an ear out for danger. Sometimes, we played a little rough with Momma's ears, and she would get mad. I remember biting Momma's ear once really hard; just once. Momma yelped, jumped, grabbed me by the neck, and pinned me down. I was so scared! Then she released me and purred. All was okay. Phew! I was more careful with Momma's ears after that. But my brothers and sister all had to learn like I did. Poor Momma's ears! Oh, and her tail too!

As I think back, whenever Momma played with us she was teaching us skills like hunting and tracking. We'd play hide and seek in the bushes. I was always amazed how well Momma could hide behind a bush. When it was our turn to hide, she would turn around and let us run and hide. Then she would slowly turn around and look for us. Sometimes she would walk right past us. We'd be still, hardly breathing, making our hearts slow down. It was hard to keep my ears from moving, tracking her movement. Then, she would sneak up on us and touch us. We were found. When it was Momma's turn to hide, we'd turn around slowly, just like she did. But we would cheat and turn quickly. She was always gone like a fart in the wind. We didn't hear her or see where she went. She could hide in plain sight. We'd look for her and find her. She didn't go very far, but she could hide right behind the nearest bush, and we wouldn't see her.

But sometimes Momma was relaxed enough to just play. That was a lot of fun. We'd run around on the grass, chasing bugs, even the pretty ones with big wings. The best was when we would just roll around and lie in the sun. We would all play, then suddenly get sleepy. It's the way of the cat. The stone behind the bushes was great for sleeping in the sunshine.

One of my favorite memories of Momma was lying in the sunshine with her bathing me with her tongue. I could hear her purring and whispering encouragement to me. She would tell me that I was a natural leader and was the bravest of my brothers and sister. She watched me pounce on them and knew that I would soon be catching food for the family. Momma would clean me and send me on my way to lie in the sun while she moved on to one of my siblings. I could hear her whispering encouragement to them, too. Lying in the sun is so nice.

One day, after lying in the sun on the big stone behind the bushes, Momma decided to take us nearby and show us the blue pond. It was nearby, just on the other side of the wooden wall. Momma jumped up and climbed the wall. She was strong! The rest of us went under the wall, through a hole to the other side. Then we followed Momma to the blue pond. It was big! Momma told us to be careful the water was deep. Warm, white, stones that were almost too hot to stand on surrounded the pond. Momma took us over to a spot in the shade. Now we could sit and watch the pond.

Momma went over to show us how to drink from the pond safely. The water was too low to just drink from it. Momma came over to the water and lay down and dipped her paw into the water, then licked her paw. When we saw this, my sister quickly went over to the water, lay down, dipped her paw into the water, and licked her paw, then did it again. I was thirsty, so I quickly went over and dipped my paw. The water tasted strange. It smelled funny, it was pretty warm, but it still felt good in my throat. We all drank some more. After a bit, Momma told us to stop drinking and follow her. She said that this water is pretty and clean, but sometimes gave her a tummy ache if she drank too much without eating. She showed us some grass nearby to chew on to help our tummies. Momma always said that if something made us feel bad, there was usually a plant or rock that we could eat or lick to make us feel better. And it was usually nearby. She said it was a wonder of life.

Momma said that this grassy area had nice people, but that they had a little dog that would chase her, so she only came here when the dog was in the people's house. Today the people weren't home and the dog was inside the house. We could see him sleeping inside the house. I turned around to show him my backside and stuck my tail in the air. That showed him. I hope he stops chasing Momma.

Now, just over the next wooden wall is another grassy area under a big tree. In this area is another dog. That dog is outside all of the time. He barks at everything he sees. He can't roam the whole area freely, but can only run as far as the string around his neck will let him. Momma would come here to eat some food, usually if the dog was sleeping. Sometimes he would wake up and chase Momma. One time, she brought us over to the tree and taught us how to climb the wooden wall so that we could watch her eat some food. She said it was too dangerous for kittens. So the four of us stood on the wooden wall and watched her sneak up to the dog's bowl. The dog was sleeping, and she crept around the side of the people's house. We could see her, but the dog couldn't. He was sleeping.

There were people inside the house. She walked in front of where we could see into the house. They saw her! We wanted to yell to her to watch out for them, but she told us to sit and be absolutely quiet. As she crept up to the food, the people opened the door and came out. Momma froze. Then the woman started swinging a long stick at Momma. Suddenly the dog woke up, came out of his home, and looked at the woman. Then he saw Momma and started barking. The woman looked at the dog, and in that instant Momma ran as fast as she could, straight to the fence and over it. Once she was over, she called to us, and we started to try to jump down to the ground. We were high up, and it was scary. Then we heard the dog barking at us, and we leapt for our lives!

We were on the ground on the opposite side of the wooden wall. We were hidden by bushes, but were so frightened to move that we stood still, cowering. Momma called out to us. I heard her and called back. She came to us. Were we glad to see her safe. When she came over to us, we all ran over to her and nuzzled her. Then the dog barked on the other side of the wooden wall. Momma calmed us down and said to follow her. As we stayed hidden in the bushes along the wooden wall and made our way away from the barking dog, Momma told us that she didn't have any food for us, and that we'd have to help look around to find something to eat.

Now we were hunters! I took the lead. I went straight to the area where Momma had shown me had some tasty moles. It wasn't too far from our cave and the stone behind the bushes, so if we caught it, we could quickly share our catch. I spoke too soon. None of us caught anything that day, not even Momma. Our bellies were empty when we came to the stone behind the bushes. We stayed hidden in the bushes, like Momma had taught us. It was getting late in the day.

Suddenly, the man opened the doorway from his home and came out to the place where he put food for us the other day. We watched quietly from the bushes, just a few steps away from him. He bent down and poured some fresh water into a puddle. Then he placed two different foods down on the ground. We could smell it. It was something smelly, something we hadn't tasted before. Then he went back into the house. When we saw that he had gone, the doorway had closed. It always made a loud sound when it opened and closed. We all ran out to see what he had put out.

This food was especially delicious. It was good to eat something tasty, especially when we were so hungry. After that meal, we came every day, once when the sun came up and again before it went down. We waited in the bushes for the man to feed us. Sometimes he would only come out with the food after the sun went down. After eating, we'd play or sometimes we'd get sleepy and lie down. If it was sunny, the stone behind the bushes was nice and warm. It was perfect to sleep on. Usually the man put several piles of food and some clean, cool, water to drink. Some of the food was wet and chewy. It tasted meaty. And some of the food was hard and crunchy. We all like to eat some of each. But the water was clean and refreshing, especially when it was hot outside.

One day, after eating, we went off to play. Momma was showing us how to climb over the wooden walls. We'd climb up and watch the dog next door. At first he didn't see us, but after a little while he noticed us and came running over. One of my brothers and sister jumped off the wooden wall, but Momma and I stayed up and watched him run around barking at us. Momma had a smile on her face. She liked teasing the dog. I'll remember that for as long as I live.

When we were heading back to the stone behind the bushes, we heard my sister and brother calling to us. We ran to see what was the matter. There, on the stone, was the strangest looking thing I had ever seen. It was sitting near the food that the man had just put out. At first, I thought it was a part of the house, but I could see that it was just sitting near the food. I could see my sister and brothers coming up to it and smelling it. Momma warned us to be careful. It wasn't an animal although it smelled like a strange cat, different from any we had smelled before. It moved when we touched it, but it wasn't alive. It was about as tall as we were when we stretched out to touch the top of it. It was the same size in every direction and had some opening big enough for us to go inside and see what it was. It was in the sun, so it was getting warm.

We had forgotten about the food. But now we couldn't resist any longer. We ate the food and drank some fresh water. When we were full, we went over to the strange thing and began to touch it. One of my brothers was brave and went inside one of the openings. He looked inside and carefully smelled it. He came out and said that it was empty. The inside was warm and soft, not hard, like the stone. After that, we each took a turn going inside and smelling it. Momma finished eating and came over to look at the strange thing. She smelled its outside then looked inside, carefully smelling it. It smelled like a cat. But she sensed no danger, so she let us keep going inside of it.

The next morning, it was still there. The man came out and put some food down, then he moved the cube back to where it was on the stone before and went in the house. After eating, we started to explore the strange cube again. This time, I was sitting inside of it. I could hear my brothers pouncing on top. Then the top of the cube came down on me. I could see my brother sliding off of the cube's top, then looking at me inside the cube, he stopped and jumped in with me. We rolled inside the cube, and the cube rolled on the stone with us inside of it. We jumped out of the cube onto the stone.

That was fun. "Let's do it again!" We jumped into the cube and started chasing each other, running inside and out. My other brother and sister saw us and joined in.

There were times when Momma went hunting or exploring at night and during the day, when she knew we were asleep and hidden in the bushes. Sometimes we'd sneak away when she was gone. Sometimes we'd follow her when she wasn't looking. She would jump a wooden wall and be gone. By the time we got over or under a wooden wall, she'd be gone. Then we'd play or go exploring. Sometimes we would stay and play longer than Momma was out, and she would return and find one or two of us missing. She'd come looking. Sometimes, when the man put the food out and we'd rush to the food, Momma or one of my brothers was still out exploring. He'd show up later and eat some of the crunchy food because we had finished the chewy food.

One night, momma came back to where we were sitting and told us not to go to where the man was putting down food. She said that there was another animal there, and that it wasn't safe to go there. Momma warned us that this animal could hurt us and that we'd have to wait. It was eating our food. I could hear my belly making noises. I was hungry from all of the playing we did that day. Momma took us a little closer to where the man put the food on the stone behind the bushes. We sat waiting. Suddenly it wasn't dark anymore, and the door opened and the man came out quickly. He had a long stick with him. He came over to where the food was. We could hear him yelling, then we saw the beast with red eyes come running away through the bushes and over the wooden wall. We sat waiting for a while. Then the man came back out and put down more food. We ran over to it as soon as he went inside. It was yummy! That beast didn't ruin our dinner after all. So the man and Momma both chased the red-eyed beast; interesting.

When the man put out our food in the morning and evening, he would move the cube back near the food. We'd spend lots of time playing. When that stone got warm from the sun, that cube was so nice to lie in. We'd curl up inside and sleep all together, safe.

I remember one of the scariest days of our young lives. It was when my brother, not the orange one, disappeared. We though he was killed or eaten by a hawk. Momma was so worried. That was the day he decided that he was able to go hunting by himself. He left the cave early. Momma was out scouting for food. When she came back, she was worried. He wasn't where she had left him! Momma asked us where he was. My sister mentioned that he went out to hunt for food. Now Momma got really worried. She looked out of the cave to make sure it was safe, then bolted out to look for him. She told us to stay where we were. She said it in a tone that let us know she wasn't playing around. We stayed there.

Momma was out for a while; the sun had moved to where it was starting to shine into the cave. Momma came back sad. She hadn't found him. We all came to her and told her we'd help find him. She took us to where the man placed the food and we waited. The sun had warmed the cube, so we played in it. Then the man came out and brought some food. We ate hungrily. We could hear the people saying things loudly from inside their home. They sounded worried too. When we were done eating we played some more, then left. Momma kept looking for my brother. We called out to him, but never heard an answer.

That night, we slept so poorly. Momma was out most of the night looking for him. We were worried about both Momma and our missing brother. Every time a dog barked or a loud noise happened we jumped. The next day came. Momma was with us. We hadn't heard her come back. We were all tired. As the sun started to rise higher in the sky, our missing brother peeked into the cave. He gave a strange meow. He had something in his mouth. It looked like a dead snake! He had caught a snake and killed it! He let it fall out of his mouth. Momma both scolded him for leaving and praised him for his catch. The snake didn't taste that good, but we still ate it. It wasn't that fresh. He wanted to tell us about his adventure, but he got silent and just curled up and slept. He never did tell us what happened that night. But he was always a little more jumpy after that. Something happened while he was gone. Someday he'll tell us.

Some days it would rain a lot. Momma would take us out away from our home underground and under some thick bushes to stay dry. She told us how important it was to keep warm and dry. We'd curl up together to stay warm. When it rained a lot, I would think of that time when we were under the big white stone, watching the water rise, and how scared we were. When the man would put the food out, we made sure to stay in the bushes near the stone and wait. It was nice to eat tasty food when it was cold and wet. The big stone behind the bushes was also dry, unless the air was moving around quickly. I could see the man or the woman watching us through the clear opening in their home. I could see the little people watching us, too, and the two cats. It was then that I realized that the little people were their children and that the woman was their Momma. The man was their Dad. They were a family, just like us!

Most of our time was spent with Momma. Sometimes we'd see another cat, a big black cat. Momma would say that he was our Dad. He stayed away from us, as Momma growled at him when he came too close to us. We didn't see him much. I do remember seeing him in the underground home sometimes. But as time went on, we saw less and less of him. That was okay; we had Momma! Little did I know that that was about to change, too.

It was a nice sunny start of the day. The man had just put food down. We had all eaten. I noticed that the man was putting out more food for us. He put out more of the crunchy food and more of the soft chewy meat. Momma went off to explore. My brothers and sister stayed on the big stone behind the bushes. It was nice and warm. The cube was also warm and toasty. After playing with the cube and rolling around inside it and on it, we all settled down for a nap inside the cube. It was a nice, cozy place. It also had two openings to get out. Momma always taught us to make sure there were two ways out, in case an animal blocked one. The cube was pushed down from the top, and we were all settled in sleeping in a pile together.

5 Sneak Attack

Suddenly, everything started moving. The openings closed, and we were flying in the air inside the cube. I awoke my brothers and sister with a yell. "Wake up, something's wrong" I meowed. We were being carried, just like Momma used to carry us when we were little. All of a sudden one of the openings opened, and we fell onto a cold floor. That made us aware of our surroundings. Momma always told us to know what was around us. We saw the man. He had come and taken the cube, with all of us inside. He put us into a bigger metal cube! This one had many openings that we could see through, but not get through. He closed the cube opening. We were trapped! Not me. I saw an opening and ran for it. My brothers and sisters were all trying to find a way out too. We were all climbing the insides of the cube, even the top.

I bolted for the opening I saw and leapt out of the cage. I was out before the man could react to block the hole. I was free! Where was I? It was dark, scary, and smelly. It reminded me of our underground home, our cave! Where was Momma? I ran as fast as I could. I found a place to hide as far away from the man and his cage. I could hear him yelling at my brothers and sister. They were still inside the cage. He blocked the opening in the cube that I escaped through. I stopped looking. I was so scared. I could hear him moving things that I had never seen before. He was strong. He could pick up things and move them. He was looking for *me*! I scrunched down as low as I could. I could hear him nearby. Then he would move away. I could hear my brothers and sister crying out for Momma. Where was she?

The man went away; I could hear him talking. Then, he came back, moving closer. I could hear him moving things. He was looking for me again. He was very close. I had found a good hiding spot. It was a little tunnel covered up and hard to find. He was nearby. I could hear him breathing. Then, the cover on top of me moved. There he was! He was big! I was frozen still with fear! He reached out with his paw and grabbed my back! I'd kill him! I'd kill him, and rescue my brothers and sister!

I attacked! I reached around and tried to bite him. I tried to scratch him. I felt some of his skin slice as I dug in with a claw. Then I saw him move his other hand near me. It would be the last thing he did. I opened my mouth and bit him with all of my strength. Claws, teeth, everything went into my attack. His paw was bigger than me. But I was the fastest and strongest of all of my siblings. I would win! I could hear him yell as my teeth sunk into his flesh. I could see and taste blood. Ha! First blood! Suddenly, he dropped me. I won! I landed on the cold metal floor. Inside the metal cage, it was a prison, with only one opening, and the man had closed it before I landed on the cold floor. I was inside the cubed cage. I hissed and yelled at the man. I ran looking for the hole, but it was blocked. I was frantic. Where were my brothers and sister? What had he done with them?

Then I saw them. They were hiding in a small cave inside the big cage. I ran to them. I was happy to see them. What had happened? Why had the man attacked us? Where was Momma? Where were we? We were all safe together. The man had left as soon as I was inside the cage. I could see him holding his hurt paw. He would remember me for as long as he lived, which wouldn't be long, if I could help it! My brothers and sister were scared and hiding inside the small cave. It was safer when we were together. There was only one way in and out of the little cave, but we would all face the opening and attack anyone who tried to hurt us. We cried out for Momma. I thought I heard her call back. Where was she? Momma!

We all lay down inside the small cave, listening for Momma, listening for the man, and hearing our hearts racing. The man came back to look at us. He spoke softly, but with tension in his voice. I saw that he had something white on his hand. It was not bleeding. Too bad! He looked at us, then placed some food and water in our cage. He went away. We could hear him walking and talking farther away. Then the whole dark wall began to make a loud noise and open to the sunlight.

We could see the outside; it was still daylight. We had to get out. The man met a woman, and together they came to our cage. She kneeled down to look at us, hiding inside the small cave inside the bigger cage. She talked to us in a quiet voice. She opened the cage door and came in closer. She reached into our cave. We hissed at her. We wouldn't let her touch us. She backed away. They closed the cage and stood there talking. I could see the man showing the woman his paw. He would remember me! They left, closing the wall behind them. It made a large clang when it closed. We were inside the man's house! Momma wouldn't be able to find us.

Later that day, the man came back with another woman, the mother of the house. She looked at us and spoke in a quiet voice. Our hearts weren't racing as fast as before; we had settled down some. Then the little boy and girl came over to see us. They were loud and made squealing noises as they looked in at us. Then after they all finally left, I went out to explore our cage. I found a place to pee and took care of that, burying it in the strange sand. Then I smelled the food and walked over to it. By that point, my sister also came out of the little cave to see the cage. She also smelled the food and came out to see what smelled so good.

We were hungry and scared and missed our Momma. But we had each other. After I ate some food, I went inside the small cave to see my brothers. One, the orange one, was awake and got up to eat some food. My other brother was too scared to come out and stayed curled up. He was shaking. I lay on top of him, to warm him, and, so he could warm me. I was scared, too. Momma would come and rescue us.

The man came again, bringing more food, water, and scraping the sand where we peed. The sand felt funny and smelled strange, sweet, like a flower, except when we peed in it. It was dark, and night came. I thought I heard Momma calling out to us. We all cried out to her as well. I think she was right outside the big metal door that opened so loudly. She was definitely there. We all cried out to her. We could hear her reassuring call to us. She would rescue us and kill those evil people, especially that man!

Momma would call out to us during the night, and we'd cry back to her. This way she knew we were still alive. When morning came, the man came out and opened the big door. We could see daylight! Was he going to let us go? Momma had hidden away in the bushes near the big door. The man opened our cage and put down more food and clean water, and scraped the sand. We were all curled up with each other in the little cave inside the bigger cage, which was inside the big room with the metal door that opened loudly. When he left us, the big door closed again.

Momma stayed in the bushes, waiting for the right time to save us. After the door closed, we were alone again. We each came out to eat, drink, and pee. The top of our little cave was soft. It was a good place to sit and watch. The big room we were in had one of those loud metal machines that the people would get into, the ones we saw them come out of when we were hiding in the bushes. Those machines were hot and smelly, and loud. The smell was pretty nasty. It smelled like some of the black sticky rocks we saw by the big white stone that the machines and people ran on. Now we had to smell it all of the time.

The next morning, after the man gave us some food and water, the woman we saw him with after he took us prisoner brought a smaller cage. While we were all hiding in the little cave, the man closed the door to the cave. Then we were up in the air. We floated out of the smelly room, deeper into the house where the people lived. The little cave landed in another cage. The man opened the door. This is what they saw, all of us huddled together in the little cave.

The woman tried to touch us; we hissed at her. We scared her off. We wanted our Momma so badly. That same day, the man moved us again, this time back to the same cage we were in before, but this time, inside the house, in a small room. At least it didn't smell bad. But, it didn't smell good either. There were strange cats just outside of the door to the little room. We could hear them and see their shadows. I imagined that they were the evil beasts that scared us when we were little. Where was Momma?

One day. There was a bunch of noise just outside the door to our little room. The door opened, and the man came in. He closed the door on the little cave and lifted us out of the cage. He took us out of the closet, then opened the door to the little cave and reached in to grab us. He grabbed me pretty easily. There was another man with him who put some strange tasting liquid in our mouths. Then he poked me with something sharp on my back. Then he placed me back in the cage.

Next he did the same to my orange brother. My other brother was next, but he got the liquid and the poke in the back, but he hissed loudly. But I was proud of my sister. She attacked them when they tried to grab her. She bit and scratched with all of her might. And she hissed so loud, even I was scared. They didn't poke her or give her the liquid. Instead, they bled! Both of them! The men quickly put us back into the little cave, then back into the cage. They were holding their paws and covering their hands. Their blood was all over the floor!

At least the little room wasn't too cold anymore. Before the man took us, it was getting cold at night, but the sun was so warm during the day. We missed the sun while we were in the little room. Sometimes the people would take us out of the cage and walk around the inside of their house; we could see the sun outside. They would come to the little room many times a day, and even at night when it was dark. They would take us out of the cage and hold us. They were nice and warm. I could hear their hearts beating. It reminded me of Momma. We'd fall asleep many times while they were holding us. They weren't as bad as I thought.

Each of the people was different. The children liked to hold us and talk to us. The boy was fun to cuddle with. Sometimes he would have all of us on top of him. The girl gave us lots of love and attention. She was gentle with us. The mother held us and talked to us. She knew how to scratch behind our ears and cuddle us. The man liked to hold us and let us sleep on him. They all knew how to make us purr.

Not long after we were getting used to the family, the man who gave us the liquids and poked us came back to give us more liquid and poke us some more. This time we didn't make him bleed. His paw had healed. After he was done poking us, he placed each of us in a new cage that wasn't in the little room; it was in the center of the people's house. We could see the sun, and we could see everything that was happening in the house. This cage was bigger and had lots of fun things to play with, and jump around into. The man would open the cage on the bottom and give us new food and water, and take away our poop and pee. Very nice! But now we could see the two cats that we smelled and heard behind the door in the little room. Now those two cats could see us, too. They were big, bigger than Momma. They were stupid. They would walk around the cage and try to smell us, then hiss.

The cage had some nice cushions to sit and sleep on almost like little nests. The room was nice and warm. It was cold outside now. I hope Momma is all right. We hadn't heard her in a while. The people were always opening the cage and holding us. I liked that. When they would come to the cage, I would run up to the door and look at them. The man had found the cube that was outside. It was clean and smelled different; not unpleasant, but different. He put it into our cage. Now we had a fun place to sleep huddled together and to play games with. I loved to climb inside the cage and jump up, then down. The cage was big enough that we could chase each other inside it.

The people would come to the cage and pick us up. Like I said, I was always running to the cage door. I liked being out of the cage, and I kind of liked the people. The people holding us were warm. They did smell funny. A lot of times, they would pick my orange brother and me. My other brother and sister weren't as happy to be held. When I was put back into the cage, I would sit on the highest part and watch over my brothers and sister as they slept in the cube. I often thought of Momma.

Sometimes I thought I could hear her outside. I could see the man put food out every night and every morning for her, just as he did for us, but I would never see her, until one night. It was after the people went to sleep and all was quiet. The two stupid big cats that were free to walk around the house were asleep, too. I could hear the wind howling outside. The man had put the food out for Momma earlier. I was asleep, but always on guard for any noise. I thought I heard Momma's cry. I opened my eyes, and there she was!

She was standing up on her back paws, looking in the window. She looked different. Her winter fur had grown in. Ours, inside this house, had not. It wasn't cold inside the house at all, but it was winter outside. Momma, I cried out! My brothers and sister awoke, and we were all looking at her. She saw us and cried out to us. Oh Momma, how I wished we were together. At that moment, I wanted to be with her. She cried out some more. She stood on her back paws and looked in at us. Suddenly there was a clicking noise, and it was dark outside. I could see her outline by the window, then as suddenly as she appeared, she turned and went off. Momma!

After that night, I always stayed alert for any sign of Momma. Sometimes I would see her, just like that first night. But many nights I would miss her. As time went on, I wished she was here with us and stopped wishing to be with her outside. It looked nasty outside, especially when the wind howled. We could feel the wind blow into the house from the doorway the man used to feed Momma. It was nice to be warm, cuddled with my brothers and sister, in the cube. And the people were nice to us. I loved to be held by them. And when they held us, they would let us go to explore the room. Sometimes we'd get to see other parts of this big house.

The people talked to us. Of course, we couldn't understand them. But it was fun to try to guess what they were saying to us. Sometimes it seemed like we were so close to understanding them, but most of the time they spoke with such strange sounds. They were loud and sometimes hurt our ears. Whenever they picked my up, they would call me "Patches" or "Patchy." When they picked up my sister, they would call her "Sabrina" or "Brini." My orange brother was called "Apricot" or sometimes "Appy," and my bigger brother was called "Mickey." We started to respond to these names.

The two big cats outside of our cage were called "Koko" and "Tigger." Koko was a big black and gray tabby cat, like Sabrina, but he had white paws. Tigger was a smaller all-gray cat. They both always came over and looked in at us. Koko would hiss a warning at us to stay away from him, but then he would always move on. Tigger would sit near our cage and watch us. He rarely hissed.

The cage was in a central part of the house. Sitting on the top perch I could see the door that the man always used to feed Momma; the main door that the people used to leave the house in the big noisy metal thing, and the door that the people used to go to the grassy area by the far side of the house. Also, we could see all that was happening in the house during the day. At night, the people slept in other parts of the house. The children slept in the higher part of the house and the mother and father slept in another part of the house, down below.

To get to the upper part of the house, the people climbed up a long climbing wall, using their feet. We could clearly see that wall from our cage. The two cats went up there to relieve themselves. Sometimes the people would let us run up that climbing wall to see what was in the upper part of the house. When they would let me out of the cage and let me run free, I would run and check out the upper part of the house. I found where the two cats went to the bathroom. There were other rooms with large strange square open places to play and hide. That room would be worth exploring sometime.

Back to our cage. There was room to jump and chase each other. There were lots of shiny and noisy things that hung from the top of the cage. We each loved to swat at them and grab them with our paws and mouths. It was fun to sit and watch the people moving around. Many times during the day, they would come to pick us up. My brother Mickey and sister Sabrina were more scared to be picked up than I was. They would hide in the cube and hiss.

Twice a day, and sometimes more, the man would bring us food, just like when we were outside with Momma. This food was tasty. We'd all run down quickly to the food bowls. Each of us gently (sometimes) nudged each other out of the way. After eating, we'd go rest in the cube or on a higher perch. This is how we spent our days, playing in our cage, eating, chasing each other, pooping, and watching the people and two cats outside of the cage. For me, I loved playing with my brothers and sister. But I also loved playing with the people. They would love us and play with us. They were nice and warm. I would fall asleep on them, getting more and more comfortable as time went on.

My sister was more scared than I was at first, but she started to like the people, too. When they would take her out to play, she would try to hide in the cube, but then they would have her, and she would relax and play. My brother Mickey was still scared. It's funny, he's the biggest of the kittens, and the most scared. I'm the smallest and the bravest. When we weren't sleeping, we were playing.

The cage had many fun toys to play with. There were lots of toys hanging from the top of the cage. We would swat at them until we knocked them off the string they were on. Then we could throw it around the cage. There was a climbing wall that I would grab onto and pull myself up to the top perch. On that level, there were beds to sleep on. And then there was the cube! We played in it, on it, and around it for hours, eventually falling asleep inside. We were warm and we had plenty to eat. We were together, but still missed Momma.

The man was spending more and more time upstairs. Sometimes he would go there for hours at a time. I could hear him making noises, loud bumps that we could feel through the cage floor, and making sliding sounds. Sometimes he would let out a yell. It sounded like he got hurt. At other times, the whole family was up there. They were carrying strange cubes up and down the stairs. Our cage was at the bottom of the stairs, so we had a front row seat to this adventure. This went on for several days. What were they doing up there?

6 Our New Room

Then, suddenly, the people came to our cage, the whole family. Each of them took one of us in their hands. This didn't happen very often, because my brother Mickey didn't like to be held that much. Anyway, they grabbed us and carried us up the stairs into the room that they were making all of those noises in. We had seen that room sometimes, when the people brought us up there to play. But now the room was messy. There were cubes all over the place. They brought us into another room, next to the messy one. It was a blue room with a large bed in it. They each came in, closed the door behind us, and put us down. We were no longer in the cage.

They all stood there or sat there watching us, smiling. The boy, Nicholas, was especially happy to see us. This was his bedroom. That's what all the noise was about; the people were moving around those cubes, making the mess. There was much to explore in the new room. There was a new covered litter box, a new climbing tree that was right by the window. I ran to it and looked out. It was sunny. The sun felt warm on my face. My sister Sabrina was on top of the bed. She smelled something. My brother Mickey went behind the bed I could see him looking out from under it. That looked like fun. My other brother was inside the litter box. It figures!

I ran over to the back side of the bed and looked around. The area under the bed was part empty and part full. It had another bed under the top bed. Mickey had found himself a nice dark "cave" to sit in between the two beds. I slipped in next to him. This space reminded me of the cave Momma had brought us to. But this floor was so soft and felt smooth. And sitting next to Mickey, it was warm. I thought of Momma outside, in the cold. I felt my sister and my other brother slipping in together. We all felt comfortable here, in this new cave, under the bed, in the boy's bedroom, on the second floor of the people's house, with a large stone "porch" behind the bushes. We slept.

It was a little while later that the door opened and the man and the boy brought some food to us. They placed it down next to a big bowl of water. I hadn't noticed it before. We all ran over to the food. It was yummy! There was a strange covering on the floor by the food bowls and the litter box. It was soft and warm, but felt sticky. It was like the floor of the old cage, but different. If I stayed on it too long, my paws would get sweaty. It had a strange pattern that was very different from the rest of the floor.

The man stayed in the room. After we ate, he sat on the floor, watching us explore the room. This was so big compared to the cage. The top of the room was so high, and there were shiny shadows dancing on it. The sun was still shining through the window. I jumped up onto the flat part by the window and looked out. We were higher up than I had ever been. I could see many houses across the big white rock. There was a tree near the window, and I could see right into it. I could hear a bird moving in the tree. Then I saw movement between the branches.

The sun felt extra fine! I heard and felt movement behind me. My sister had climbed up the climbing tree behind me. She was at the top and stared down at me. I could see her smile; she was the first to the top. My orange brother jumped up on the flat part by the window, next to me. I settled down to soak up some sun. I looked around; all four of us were sitting in the sun. How we had missed the sun while we were in the cage.

All of this time, the man just sat there and watched us. He looked both happy and sad. I remember thinking what was going through his mind. I went over to him, crawled on top of his belly, and settled in. I noticed my sister came over. She curled up just below me. My brother Apricot settled on top of his paws. Mickey was too shy to come on top of the man, but lay down near the man, purring. We were all purring, even the man!

This room was fun to explore. There were hiding places all over; under the bed, on top of the bed, under these soft comfortable mounds (blankets). There were more places to sit and watch my brother or sister walk by and surprise pounce on them. The climbing tree was right next to the window, where we would sit in the sun and watch people walk by outside with their stupid dogs on a string. Sometimes I could hear them barking at something near the house. Momma! I hated those dogs. Leave my Momma alone!

There were other big wooden things in the room. One of these was near the bed, and we could walk over to it, walk on top of it, and go over to two other wooden things. They were smooth and flat, and smelled and looked funny; not unpleasant, but funny. The top was a little slippery. It had a strange shiny back part to it that was different. It made e room look a lot bigger, like there was a whole new section to explore. But it just looked that way. I couldn't go through it. And whenever any of us walked up to it, we would see a kitten that looked like us. But there was no kitten there. It was so weird.

Anyway, we passed the big shiny wall on the way to the tall wooden thing. It had lots of places to hide and jump onto. One time the man came into the room. We could always hear him walking to the door. He came in, looked around. Suddenly he got a worried look on his face. He was looking for us! He found three of us, but was busy trying to find my brother, Apricot. Appy was hiding inside the big wooden thing. He was in plain sight, but he fit perfectly inside an opening in the tall wooden thing. He was standing still, blending in. Then the man saw him. I could tell he relaxed. He laughed and smiled.

When we were by ourselves, we would jump all over the room. We did that when the people were in the room, too. It was especially fun when the boy came in to sleep at night, or the man came in and lay on the bed with the sun shining on him. They were nice and warm, and we would all curl up on them, or next to them, and sleep, too. It was like sleeping all curled up with my brothers and sister, but with a much bigger kitten warmer.

We spent many days in that room. We each had our favorite spots. Mickey and Appy liked to sleep between the beds. It was dark, safe, and comfortable. Sabrina liked to sleep with them, as well as on top of the bed with me. If the sun was shining through the window, onto the bed, then we all slept in the sun. The climbing tree by the window was covered with the same covering as the main floor. It was soft to walk on and easy to sink your claws into. Perfect for climbing fast. It was a lot of fun to climb up and race down, chasing each other.

When the sun shone on it, it was the perfect place to sleep. It had two cozy flat places big enough for us to cuddle together and sleep.

The other thing we could do now was play. We had a lot more room to chase each other. We had room to jump at full stride. And we took advantage of this. We practiced stalking each other, quietly waiting for my brothers or sister to emerge from under the bed then jumping from the furniture to the bed, and back, and chasing each other all around the room. Of course, I was the master hunter. Sometimes I would sit so long, waiting for one of my siblings to come out, I would fall asleep.

The bed was comfortable, with lots of soft fluffy room to curl up on. A couple of times a day, the man would come up and sit with us. He would bring us food or fresh water, then sit down and watch us. Usually I was the first to go over to him, to see what he was doing. I would jump up to his lap, then crawl onto his chest and nuzzle him. Then my sister would be there right next to me. Then Appy would sit on his legs. Mickey would sit nearby. He was scared of the people's touch. The rest of us were getting more and more comfortable, especially with the man.

There were times when he would come up during the day and lie on the bed. The sun would be shining on the bed, and he would lie there, waiting for us to hop onto him. He was so warm and soft. We would all run onto the bed when he lay down. It was a battle between my sister and me as to who got to sit closest to his head. She would settle down on top of his side. Appy would be on his legs, Mickey on a pillow nearby, and me, as close to his head as I could. I would cuddle up to him and fall asleep right away.

Lying on top of the man was kind of a sport between my sister and me. She was becoming comfortable with the human family, too. We loved when the other people came into our room. They knew how to hold us and how to scratch us just right. It felt so nice. I only wished Momma could be there with us. It was still cold outside. We could tell because the window felt cold, and a little wind would blow by the window. We could feel the cold and were happy to be warm inside. Sitting by the window became one of our favorite things to do. Oh, how we had missed the sun. Now, we had a room with a view!

The man had put in a new litter box. This one came with a cover and a door. We would walk in, look around, and walk out. The door would swing in and out for us. Soon, I discovered how much fun it was to stalk a sibling while he/she was pooping. I could hear him/her burying their poop, then the door would start to swing open. I would leap into action, startling my brother or sister. Of course, they quickly learned to copy the master. It got to the point that I had to be careful coming out of the potty!

The other members of the human family came in to see us and play with us a lot. They gave us lots of love. They even played hide and seek. Mickey was the best at hide and seek. He would mostly hide, but sometimes he came out to play as well. It was playtime, with my new family!

Although we spent most of our time in our new room, we did get out sometimes to play in the room next door. This was the room with all of those square cardboard boxes, filled with lots of strange things. This room also had lots of small interesting things to sniff, bite, pull, and bat around. Some of those things were sitting on a shelf pretty high up from the floor, perfect for climbing. And what man places up high might just come down by the will of a cat! This cat!

I'm climbing along a high dangerous ledge high above the floor below. This cat is stalking the unsuspecting prey, his unsuspecting sister. He pauses when she does. He readies to pounce on her, crouching, waiting, and leaping. And with perfect precision, fur goes flying. I love stalking Sabrina! Or Mickey, or Apricot! But then, after I surprise Sabrina, she turns and stalks me. That's how the game is played. Now the hunter is hunted. Not for long!

This room had a lot of things to play with. There were lots of little things high up on ledges that were great to climb on, pounce from, and drop things from. Cats are born with an uncanny understanding of gravity. We show this ability every time we are dropped. We *always* land on our paws. We like nothing more that to demonstrate how to best use gravity. Just watch us. It's so much fun simply helping things fall. Sometimes the people would yell at us. I'm not sure why. If they didn't want us cleaning their room, they should have cleaned it themselves. Did I mention, we cats like our places clean? And, unlike our room, this room was a mess. It was filled with boxes, things to chew on, things to bat around, and best of all, great places to hide.

The playroom had lots of boxes stored in it. There were open boxes, too. They were perfect places to explore and hide in. In one corner was a blue chair that the people sat in sometimes. We all liked to go underneath the chair. It was dark and smelled funny. There was lots of moving metal strings that made loud screechy noises when the chair moved. I didn't like it much, but I had to check it out. Mickey liked to hide underneath the chair. He hid there when the people corralled us back into our room. They would call him and try many ways to get him to come out. He is the best at hiding.

Sometimes a bright dot would appear near us and move around quickly. It was irresistible. I think the people liked it, too, because they would laugh out loud whenever it appeared. It would whirl around quietly. I would pounce on it, and it would jump on my paws. Then it would jump away, into our room. The people would close the door behind us. We would always wait by the door until all of us were in the room. Family sticks together. I mentioned that Mickey is a good hider, but even he couldn't resist the red dot. Soon, he would join us. Then it was time to play in our room.

Right next to the playroom was a smaller room that had fresh water in it. I could smell it. That's the room where the two other cats went to the bathroom. Sometimes one of us would go in there and pee in their litter box. Kittens rule; old cats have to bury the pee!

When it got dark, the people would come in and make it light in the room. They touched a white little stick on the wall, and there was light. If it was dark, we were probably sleeping, and the light would wake us up, although we could always hear and feel the people coming. They're loud, even when they think they're quiet. They would be bad hunters and would go hungry.

So I studied the stick on the wall that they touched to make it light. But my brother, Apricot, studied the door. Smart kitten! He always would tell us that he was figuring out how to open the door so we could get out. And sometimes he did it! Somehow he reached under the door and pulled. We heard it make a click then open. Sometimes he's a goofball, but he's my smart goofball brother. And he opened that door.

We carefully peeked out from our room. The playroom looked the same; no people there, no other cats. He really opened the door! We could hear the people's voices downstairs. There were other voices, too. They were coming from that strange noisy box by the wall. It was loud and made lots of movement. Sometimes, when we were sitting with the people, that box would be on. At first, when we were younger, it hurt our ears. As we got older, we got used to it.

We slowly crept out of the room, looking around the playroom. With no one to stop us, and the door open from the playroom, we could explore the upper part of the house on our own. Then we went out on the area above the stairs where you could look down on the lower area. Slowly we kept on going. Apricot and I led the way. Sabrina followed closely. Mickey hid under the blue chair. As we moved out, the people didn't see us. But someone else did. The big cat Koko was sitting at the top of the stairs. He was looking the other way and did not see us. Yet. Then, just as we saw him, he turned his head and saw us. He hissed loudly. He put his ears back; I knew he was mad, or maybe just not happy. The people had heard Koko's hiss and looked up at us. They yelled and started to run up the stairs toward us. We ran back away from them, into our room. They took some time to find Mickey. They eventually did find him, and the bright dot appeared again, and soon Mickey joined us. That was fun! We'll have to try that again.

One of the best things about our new room was the sleeping arrangement. We were no longer in the tiny cage, but had so many places to sleep. We had a choice, on the windowsill, in the sun, on the climbing tree, under the big bed in the dark safe place, on the floor, which was so soft, or on top of the big bed, which was soft and warm, especially when the sun was shining on it. We got the chance to feel fully rested during the day, so that we could party at night. And party we did!

Cats are nocturnal by nature. We didn't really know this yet. We were still kittens. But we weren't tiny kittens, like when we were captured and brought into the house by the man. We were older kittens. And we were starting to appreciate the fun of playing at night. Nicholas, who came to sleep in our room every night, complicated our nighttime activities. Okay, technically it was his room that we were living in. Anyway, he would come up with some of his family at bedtime. They stayed for a while, played with us (that was a lot of fun). Then they turned off the light and left Nicholas and us four to go to sleep. That was our cue to curl up and sleep for the night.

Of course, as we grew older, we weren't as tired; after all, we slept a lot during the day. In fact, the four of us wanted to play. And we did! As soon as the door closed and the footsteps receded, we would play tag, or hide and seek, or pounce on a sensitive part of Nicholas and watch him jump. That last one was a game we discovered by accident, but it became a favorite. One of the best nighttime games was who could make the smelliest poop in the litter box. Apricot was the reigning champion. I could see the smile on his face when he came out of the litter box. Of course, nighttime was the perfect time to have a snack. Our human family made sure we had plenty of dry food for the night. That was thoughtful of them. It crunched particularly loudly and echoed in the room when all was quiet at night.

These were fun times in the room. We were bonded with our new family, although, I still thought about Momma outside in the cold while we were warm. I found myself thinking about her less and less, mostly when I was sitting on the windowsill, and I would see a human walking a dog on the string. The dog might bark at the bushes below us. Stupid dog! Poor Momma. She was free; free to be cold, hungry and scared, while we were warm, fed, and maybe not as free, but happy. Yes, we were happy with our new family.

All was going well. We were happy in our room. The people came in one day and collected us again. But this time, they put all of us in a smaller cage. We were scared and meowed. We asked them "What are they doing with us?" The man carried the cage in his hand and put us into the metal rolling thing. We were now inside, along with the boy and girl. The metal thing made a loud noise and started to shake. I could see through the cracks in the cage. We were outside, and we were moving!

The four of us were huddled together in this small cage. We were scared, but glad to be with each other. It was reassuring to hear my siblings breathing, even though I knew we were all scared. The metal thing was loud and shook as it moved. It also smelled unpleasant. I don't think the people riding with us were worried about the noisy car we were in. Instead, they were focused on looking at us in the cage. As we looked back, we could see them staring in at us.

They were saying strange things to us, in an almost condescending way. I would have to talk to Nicholas about that later. After a while, they talked less to us, and we settled down. The vibrations inside the car felt reassuring and lulled us to sleep. It wasn't a deep sleep, but we did close our eyes. Sometimes the car would shake more, and we would all open our eyes and look out the cracks. It was daytime, and we had been riding for some time.

Then as suddenly as we started, we stopped. The car stopped moving, and it stopped shaking. Nicholas and Katrina opened the doors and got out. The man did, too. He picked up the cage with us in it and took us to a nearby building. The building was awful. It smelled nasty, and there were the sounds of many animals crying and whimpering, although some were glad to see their humans. Mostly that was the stupid dogs. The man put the cage on the ground. We could see the people's feet and a couple of dogs. One looked happy to be leaving. He was all excited to see the human.

The other dog just stood there and shook. It was embarrassing. After a while, the man picked up the cage and passed us to another human. She looked in at us and smiled. I think she was glad to see us, but if I had only known then what was going to happen, I would have scratched her badly.

She put our cage down on a table and walked away. Soon, another person came up to our cage, talking to us, trying to calm us down. That's what Nicholas was trying to do to us in the car, calm us down. He should have rubbed my ears. That always works when the man does it. Surprisingly, it helped when she talked to us. But then we would hear a bark or a cry from a dog or cat nearby and we'd get all scared again. The woman who was talking to us opened the cage and reached in, not so fast. But before I could strike at her, she grabbed my brother Apricot. He was scared. She closed the cage and held him. We could see what she was doing to him. She pet him, talked to him, placed him on a raised part of the table, and when the table made a funny sound that none of us had ever heard a table make before, she talked some more to him. I could sense him tensing. I wonder what she said to him. Then, she placed Apricot in another cage.

She did that to all of us. When she picked me up, I could tell she cared about us, like our new human family, but different. She placed me on the raised part of the table. It moved a little, and then made that funny sound. She picked me up, then placed me on the table nearby. This is where Apricot tensed. What did she say to him?

I soon found out. She said nothing. Instead, I felt something strange go into my butt! Now I knew why he tensed! So did I. This isn't a funny thing for a cat to have happen to him. Humans really are strange. I felt the strange thing come out of my butt. Then she placed me in the bigger cage, along with Apricot. Soon Sabrina and Mickey would join us. None of us was happy. We were glad to see each other, but scared. Our family was nowhere to be seen. Instead, these strange people were pulling and prodding us.

The lady left us alone. We settled down, huddled together, and so scared. I think this was the most scared I had been since the first day when the man had taken us from Momma. Momma! Where are you? Help us! We all started to meow for her.

Not long after that, the lady came back and picked us up one at a time. She then placed us into a strange, clear cage. I heard a soft hissing sound and smelled a strange odor. Suddenly I was very sleepy. I looked at my brothers and sister. They were falling asleep, too. That was the last thing I remember.

I woke back up a few seconds later. I was in the cage, along with my brothers. My sister wasn't with us. What happened? I felt tired and closed my eyes for another nap. I awoke again, this time more refreshed. I felt strange. Like something was missing. My sister was still gone. That wasn't it. Something else was missing. I felt a strange pinching feeling between my back legs, just below the tail, where my blueberries used to be. Used to be! Something bad had happened! I called out to my brothers. They were waking up again, too. Their blueberries were gone, too.

The evil lady had come back. She put the three of us boys back into our cage and carried us out. The man and boy were there. The people were talking to the man. He looked worried. And Sabrina was still gone! What kind of a torture house is this? The man put our cage back into the car, and Nicholas got in next to us. He tried to talk to us in a reassuring tone. It was nice, but nothing could make us feel good right now. The ride back in the car was less eventful; we slept most of the way.

When we got back to our house, the man and Nicholas opened our cage and let us back into our room. It was nice to be back, away from those torturers. Soon, he brought us some food. It was especially tasty, and we ate till we were full. Since there were only three of us, we had more to eat. Mickey's belly looked big. Soon we lay on the bed and slept. The unpleasant feeling between my legs wasn't as strange and painful as it was before. In a couple of days I forgot about it. Later that night, we all bounced around from the bed to the table, the chair, and back again, while Nicholas tried to sleep. It was fun keeping him awake. But hey, we weren't tired!

Late the next day, the man came up to our room and brought Sabrina in the cage. He let her out. She looked wobbly, but we were so glad to see her. And she was glad to see us. She told us how she fell asleep like we did, and when she woke up, her belly was sore. She hurt inside, too. The next day, the people put her back in the clear cage and she fell asleep again. She awoke the second time and was still sore, but at least she didn't hurt as much. Then the woman came to her, put her back into a cage, and brought her back to the man and the boy Nicholas. They drove in the rolling machine, then they brought her back here to us. I could see a bunch of her belly fur was missing.

She walked funny and complained of belly soreness. She had some strange strings on her belly. Even though she was sore, she still played with us. I could tell she didn't want to jump around as much as we did, but she rolled and played anyway. After a couple of days we were all feeling better. This was a strange experience that I don't want to repeat. Since that day, we haven't been so aggressive toward each other, at least for a while. I guess that's good.

After that day, most things were normal. We spent a lot of time playing with each other, and with our new human family. As I mentioned before, Nicholas slept in the room with us. When it was time for him to wake up, the man would come in to wake him and us. That was annoying, but it always meant food. The man would come in, bring fresh food, and change our water. Nicholas would get up and say hello to us. Of course, we spent the night sleeping on and around him, so we had said hello a number of times during the night. He just slept through it, most of the time. Sometimes we would wake him up. That was always fun, because he would pop up in bed and try to figure out where he was.

At other times, we'd keep him from falling asleep. This was the best, because we liked playing with him. We'd pretend to sleep while his father or mother was in the room. But when they left the room and closed the door, we'd come out and play. Usually Sabrina and I were already on the bed, pretending to be sleepy. Apricot and Mickey were usually under the bed or sitting on the windowsill waiting for the adults to leave. When all was quiet, we'd pounce. Jumping on Nicholas was something we had to do. Usually there was some movement under the blanket, and we just had to pounce on it. Sometimes when we pounced with extreme prejudice and claws out, we'd get a little yell from him. That was a job well done. Then he would giggle, and move his feet under the blanket. Sometimes we'd pounce higher up on him, around the top of his legs. Those pounces usually resulted in lots of movement under the blanket. He would even sit up sometimes.

And, of course, we would play tag or chase at night. Apricot would blend in really well against the wood, but Sabrina would blend in best at night. But Apricot was the most vocal when we found or caught him. Mickey was starting to become pretty good at hide and seek. He could hide better than any of us. Sabrina was becoming good at stalking. I would have to watch out for her.

One time, Nicholas got up in the middle of the night, went out of the room heading downstairs. He had left the door open. We couldn't pass this up. We all crept out slowly, watching for the two stupid big cats. We explored the playroom and even went into the litter box. But then we went out farther, out to the top of the stairs, all of us, except Mickey, that is. He came out to the top of the stairs and stopped. The rest of us went down the stairs to explore the rest of the house. The cats were nowhere to be found. We saw that Nicholas had gone into the bedroom where his mother and father slept. We knew this from when we were in the little cage near their room. As we approached, we could hear voices in the room next to their bedroom. The door was open; it was pretty bright in there. We slowly crept toward the light. Then the man came around the corner and jumped back, like we had scared him. He saw us and let out a little yell. We all ran as fast as we could. Apricot ran toward the stairs, Sabrina and I went to the other side, hiding behind some big pieces of furniture that the people liked to lie down on. The man came out, then the mother. The room lit up all of a sudden. There weren't a lot of places to hide. Sabrina and I both ran toward the stairs, then up. The man came up to check on us. He took a couple of minutes chasing us back into the room. When we were all there, he closed the door and went back downstairs. That was fun!

7   Freedom! Sort of.

We had been up in our room (Nicholas's room) for quite some time. The sun was making the room warmer with each passing day. We could hear the birds in the tree every day. I even thought I heard little birds calling out to their mother for food. This made me think of Momma. From time to time, we would think about her. Sometimes, one of us might get a glimpse of her running from near our house to the one across the big white stone path where the rolling noisy metal things went.

But, as time went on, we thought less and less about her, and more and more about our new family. They loved to hold us and cuddle us. And we loved to be held and cuddled, too; except for Mickey. I knew he loved being here, with us, and with the people. He would purr loudly when one of them came up to our room. He would always come and sit near the people, but just far enough so that they couldn't grab him easily. That wasn't a problem for me, or Sabrina, or Apricot. We loved to sit on our people. Mickey just didn't want to be held by the people. I wonder what happened to him while he was away those two days?

One day, the man came up to our room with Nicholas. After playing with us, they left the door open. We went out into the adjoining playroom and checked out the big cats' litter box. The man had left the door open to the stairs and the rest of the house. He was standing right there looking at us; kind of stupidly, I might add. He could see that he left the door open. He was talking to us. Then I bolted for the open door. I was sure he would grab us like before. Not this time! I made it, and continued down the stairs. Apricot was right behind me, followed by Sabrina and Mickey. Mickey ran out, but then slowed down at the top of the stairs. The man came out near the top of the stairs and stared out at us. Mickey saw him coming toward the stairs and ran down with the rest of us. We were all out of our room and in the main part of the house. Our old cage was gone.

There was the soft couch where we sat on the human children and played. No one was chasing us. We explored the room more and more, looking behind the furniture and smelling everything. We wandered into the room where the man and mother slept. Suddenly around the corner came the big cat Koko. He looked at me and hissed, loudly. I froze. I was going to stay away from him. He didn't have to warn me. As he walked away from me and out of the room, I could hear him hissing again, this time at Apricot. Boy, that cat was unpleasant. We decided to follow him!

None of the humans tried to grab us. Instead, the man just stood there looking at us and smiling. Then we heard the magic sounds of our food being prepared. We had gotten used to this sound when we were in the little cage just a couple of steps away from where I stood. The man was preparing our food. We could hear the banging of metal bowls against the stone ledge by his waist. We stopped our exploring and started to go over to where he stood.

The two big cats were waiting on the floor near the part of the stone ledge, where the water flowed. They were hungry, too. The man walked over to them and placed a bowl by each of them. Hey, we were hungry, too! Then he came over to where we were and placed a couple of bowls of food for us. We all dove into the food. It was delicious. I think it tasted better. I remember eating the same food before, in our cage and in our room, but today it just tasted better. The four of us ate our fill. We were done before the two big cats. Appy ran over to see what they were eating, but Koko the big cat ignored him and kept eating. Appy came over and told us that they were eating the same food as we.

Now, it was time to explore! And there was so much to explore. Where to begin? After eating, I was thirsty. I hadn't seen any water bowls. Instead, there was flowing water. No kidding. Near the food bowls, on the floor, was a white fountain of flowing water. This wasn't like the flowing water fountain in the bathroom; this one was easy to get to, just by walking to it and drinking. The water tasted pretty good. It wasn't cold, but it still tasted good. When I was done, Sabrina came over and drank some, too. When she moved off, the older cat, Koko, went to the fountain and started to drink. He was strange. He would dip his paw into the water, then lick his paw, just like Momma had taught us by the pond. He did that many times. He seemed very happy drinking like that. I made a note to try that, when no one else was looking!

I noticed something strange. The people kept watching us, so they knew where we were, but they didn't chase us back to our room. The man had a satisfied look on his face. He sat on the couch. I slinked over to where he was sitting and jumped up to check him out. He was happy to see me. I came over to him, purring. He welcomed me into his arms, and I curled up on his warm body.

From my vantage point, I could see my sister stalking Apricot. This was going to be good. She had slowly moved into position. She was shaking in anticipation, about to pounce. She didn't see me. I couldn't resist. I sprung into action! It was a perfectly timed intercept. The startled look on both of their faces was priceless; my sister's from the shock of my arrival, and the man's from the surprise of my sudden departure. Always keep them guessing!

We all curled up on the couch near the family as they sat watching the magic moving window. Even one of the older cats, Tigger, came up onto the couch and settled down on top of the couch, near the mother's head. Koko stayed on the ground, warily watching us. I was surprised to see Mickey sitting near one of the people. He wasn't as close to them as we were, but for him, it was close. He was watching the magic window with great concentration. It was interesting, but not that interesting. Nap time!

So the people had let us out into their (our) house. Very interesting! Little by little the family went to sleep, first the father, then the children, and finally the mother. She obviously stayed up late to watch over the family, and when all was safe, she could sleep, just like Momma. Momma! I ran over to the widow to see if she was there. She wasn't. I could feel the rest of my brothers and sister near me, as they, too, remembered about Momma. Eventually the light went off outside. It was dark; time to explore the house.

Exploring the house was something we had all talked about doing since we were in the little cage on the ground floor. We had had chances to do that a little at a time, when the people let us out to play with them. And we know the upstairs pretty well, since they moved us to our room there. But now, we were free to roam around, except for the annoying bigger cats. Every time one of us came near one of them, they hissed loudly at us. At night they seemed to settle down in one spot. This made it easier for us to avoid them. Where to start? I saw Koko heading for the parents' bedroom. This was a perfect place to check out first.

As I walked closer to their room, I could see Koko jumping up onto their bed. He went over between the two of them and curled up. He was facing the door, obviously wanting to keep a protective eye on it. He's a smart cat. As I walked into the room, I could see another door to the right. I'll have to remember to check that out later. I could see Sabrina moving past me toward the bed. Apricot had slinked past the both of us heading straight for the far side of the bed. What was he planning? Then, I saw him disappear *under* the bed. What was going on? Sabrina saw this, too. She stopped, startled.

We called out to Appy. He called back. All was fine. We went over to where he had disappeared, and we looked under the bed. The bed was like our bed upstairs; it had room underneath to lie down. But I couldn't tell that from outside the bed; it had protective covers that went to the floor. Excellent! We had found a new hiding place. Appy was lying in the middle of the floor under the bed, probably wondering what had taken us so long to get here. Sabrina was here, too. Then it was Mickey poking his head under the bed covers, looking at us. Yes, this was a nice safe spot. We'd have to check it out in the daytime. The bottom of the bed we were sleeping under had a strange dark covering that moved when we touched it, and we could see through it a little. There was room above us. This would have to be examined later.

I could hear the man snoring on top of the bed. As I poked my head out from under the bed, I felt a strange sensation of being watched. As I cautiously started to come out from under the bed, a black ball of fur landed on me. She yelled, "Tag, you're it!" I could hear her laughing as she sprinted away. Sabrina had been on top of the bed. How did she get there so quickly, and without me noticing that she was gone? She's good! I chased her. As I sprinted out of the bedroom, I stopped to see where she had gone. Again, I felt like I was being watched. As I backed up toward the bedroom door, I ran into something furry and moving. The loud hiss made me jump. When I landed on my feet, I ran as fast as I could. The stairs were to my left.

I bolted up the stairs, past Sabrina. So that's where she was spying on me from. She ran off behind me as well. Then when I was at the top of the stairs looking back down, I could see what startled me; Koko. He'd heard us playing under the bed and came down to see what the fuss was about. I had backed into him.

At that moment, I saw the most graceful maneuver ever performed by cats. As Koko was walking out of the bedroom, but still in the doorway, Apricot and Mickey blew past him, flying through the air, just past his head, startling him, then avoiding his swats as they flew past him, safely landing on their paws and bouncing up the stairs following me. Their looks of satisfaction were absolutely indescribable. We all laughed as we stuck out our tongues at Koko. Since we were upstairs and near our room, we decided to see what was happening there, and sleep in the comfort of our old bed, with the built-in cat warmer Nicholas.

We laughed to ourselves as we came into our bedroom. All was as we had left it; our litter box, our climbing tree by the window, our water bowl. The food bowls were gone! Mickey had gone under the bed, Apricot was on the windowsill, Sabrina was drinking water, and I decided to see if Nicholas had a toe sticking out from under the blanket that would be worth pouncing on. As I jumped onto the bed, I quickly noticed something wrong. Nicholas was in bed, but where Nicholas' head was supposed to be was a big dark cat. Tigger was in our bed! He noticed me, looked up, smiled, and put his head back down on the pillow. He was curled around Nicholas' head. He wasn't stupid either. That was a very warm spot. Great. Well, I settled down on the next warmest spot. I could hear lots of purring from under the bed, the windowsill, the top of the climbing tree, and at the top of the bed. It had been a great day.

We slept well that night. The man didn't come up to our room and close the door. Instead they left it open all night. Koko came up in the middle of the night to use the litter box. At least he didn't use our litter box. I saw him come into our room. He looked around carefully, then turned around and left. He'd be back, I'm sure. I closed my eyes and slept. Nicholas didn't move around as much as he usually did, so I could settle down into a nice spot by his waist. Sabrina was sleeping nearby. Apricot was by his legs, and Mickey was sleeping in the far corner of the bed. Tigger was still by his head. I settled in.

The next morning, I was awakened to the sounds I remembered hearing when we were in the little cage. Someone, a human, was awake downstairs. This usually meant food. I looked around. Mickey wasn't on the bed. Sabrina was sleeping, but had heard the noise as well. Apricot and Tigger were still sleeping. I hopped off the bed quietly and stretched. I heard Sabrina plop down next to me. She looked at me, funny-like, and stretched as well. We started out the door toward the stairs. I heard another cat plop off the bed, Apricot. Tigger would have made a much louder plop.

As I got to the top of the stairs, I could hear someone making noise in the area where food was served to us. I hurried down the stairs eager to see who was making the noises. As I reached the bottom of the stairs I could see the man standing by the upper water dispenser drinking something and sighing. I came over by his feet and brushed by, giving my customary greeting. I started purring. He looked down, happy to see me. He reached down and picked me up.

My sister looked up at me and called to me. She knew I was happy. She liked to be held as well. The man held me, nuzzling my head to his. It was our customary greeting. I saw what he was drinking. It wasn't water, but something brown and smelled strange. I could smell it on his breath. It wasn't unpleasant, but it wasn't cold clean water either. After looking him in the eye, he put me down. As he lowered me, I slipped out of his hands, landed on my front paws, and kept on walking.

At that point, the man decided to feed us. First he went to the place where our food was kept and opened the door. He took out several small shiny round things and placed them up high, near the upper water fountain. He then proceeded to open the shiny things and placed our food in the metal bowls. Then he carried them over to where we ate. First he put a bowl down in front of the oldest cat, Koko. Then he went over to where we ate and placed the bowls for us.

As he walked over, the four of us weaved in and around his legs. It was fun and challenging at the same time. We had to pay attention to where we walked so as not to get stepped on. We meowed, calling to him. He placed the bowls with our food down on the ground right in front of us. We were hungry and ate quickly. Mickey was there, too. The only one missing was Tigger. Between bites, I could see Tigger hobbling down the stairs. He was a big fat gray cat. At least he wasn't mean. He waddled over near the kitchen, and the man walked over to him and placed his food down in front of him. Tigger sniffed the food, ate some, then walked away disgusted. Strange cat. The food was tasty.

When no one was paying attention, I walked over to his food bowl and tasted his food. It was good, even better tasting than my food. Score! I was starting to get full and decided to take a break. Koko was still eating. For an older cat, he was sure a slow eater. The only one of the four of us who was still eating was Apricot. Even Mickey was done. Apricot always liked to overeat, then he'd settle down to digest. I'd have to do that, too. Nap time!

There was a lot to explore in the house. I already mentioned the bedroom with the nice dark hiding place under the bed. That soon became our favorite hiding place, especially when something scared us. Nicholas would have friends come to the front door and make a loud ringing noise. Whenever we heard that, we'd run under the bed and peek out to see who had come into the house. A lot of times it would be other children at the door. Sometimes they would come inside and play. They would run up and down the stairs, yelling loudly to each other, just like the four of us played with each other. Other times they would sit and watch the magic moving window.

As soon as the other children would leave, we knew it was safe to come out. Koko always stood his ground whenever the doorbell rang. He was pretty fierce in protecting the house. I wish I could be that brave! But something about that doorbell just made us all run and hide. A lot of times Tigger would be under the bed with us. He didn't like the doorbell or when strange people were in the house. Out of the four of us, Mickey was the most afraid. How I wonder what happened to him when he disappeared for those two days?

Many times when the family would sit on the couches and watch the magic moving window, we'd all sit on or near them. They would be all warm and we could snuggle on them. Many times they covered themselves with large soft covers. This was especially comfortable after the sun went down. There would be two or three of us snuggled with the family. Sometimes even Mickey would come up and sit nearby.

It was still cold outside in the mornings. I could see the grass was just starting to turn green. The sun was getting stronger. We had our favorite windows to watch out into the big grassy field in back of the house. We liked to sit by the windows to get some sun, but it was exciting to sit and watch the birds fly around and the squirrels running along the top of the wooden walls. Sometimes we'd get a glimpse of Momma hunting or slinking through the grass. Sometimes we'd see other cats as well. It seems that there would always be a dog barking from beyond the wooden wall, when Momma or another cat was walking in the grass.

When we weren't watching birds or eating or sleeping, we were playing. The whole house gave us lots of room to run and chase each other. We could perfect our hunting skills. It seemed that Apricot or Mickey were our favorite prey. Apricot was pretty unobservant when he walked around the house. He was becoming easier to stalk. This didn't go unnoticed by my archrival in stalking, my sister Sabrina. There were many times I'd sit hidden, waiting for Apricot, only to be surprised by Sabrina. Sometimes she would pounce on Apricot first; at other times, she'd be stalking me. Of course, I stalked her, too. She was a pretty good hunter. There were a lot of times she would out-wait me. Of course, I was still the best.

Remember, I mentioned the second door in the mother and father's bedroom. Well, that door leads to their litter box and place where they wash themselves; oh, and the dark little room where they keep their clothes. People sure are funny that way. Well, the room where they wash themselves has a large waterfall that sprinkles rain on them. I can hear them in there washing themselves. They must like it, because whenever one of them is in there they don't seem scared or unhappy. They come out smelling different than how they went in. It's not an unpleasant smell, but it's strong, like flowers. Anyway, they go in there and get wet. Then they wrap themselves in a large cloth and dry themselves.

Personally, I prefer my tongue. It's much more pleasant than getting all wet. But the best part is when they come out of there, because I get to go in and catch some of the water. It's a lot of fun, and I get to drink my fill of fresh water and catch it with my paws and mouth. The key to catching it is patience. It doesn't always come out when I think it will. And sometimes it takes a while. But suddenly, it gurgles from the top and comes shooting out, straight down. The first time I went in there was when I was sitting nearby and it started to gurgle. I had never heard such a sound before, not in the smelly cave, not anywhere. When I ran in there, I could see water flowing down on the stone floor, then trickling into the hole in the floor. It stopped as fast as it started. I had missed it.

Sometimes, in the middle of the night the water would gurgle and flow out. A lot of times, I'd sit in the bathroom near the shower, waiting for the water to flow. I'd be dreaming about it gurgling and hitting the stone floor. I'd wake up and realize that I had just missed the water flow, and that the sounds I had dreamt were the water flowing while I slept. Cool! Other times the flow lasted for a while, and I could get to it and try to catch the water as it hit the floor. The water hits the floor and I grab it. It gets through my paws and splashes around. But I can't help myself; it's just too much fun.

Sometimes, Sabrina and Mickey are interested in catching the water, too. We'd all sit near the entrance to the waterfall area, waiting for the human to come out, so we could catch water. I'd always be the first, slipping right by the person who opened the shower door. That's what they called it, the shower. Getting in first allowed me to get the best spot right near where the water would fall. It always fell in the same spot. The stone floor felt warm whenever the people were finished with the shower. My paws and tail would get wet, but it was worth getting the prime spot.

A lot of times, the water would flow right after the people left the shower. So getting in quickly paid off. When they were with me, Sabrina would come in right after me, but Mickey was always last, waiting for the people to get far enough away before he came in cautiously. I wonder what happened to him those days he was gone. He never was the same.

Anyway, the bathroom became our favorite place to be. The floor was made of strange square stones that were a great place to cool off when we were hot. There was plenty of water to drink, not just in the shower, but there were other smaller water flows there. They flowed into big white bowls. Many times, the people would leave one of them flowing for Tigger to drink from. That was one of his favorite places to be, especially in the mornings, when the man and woman were getting ready. Sometimes the people would finish their drying, put on some clothes, and go out, but leave the water flowing for us. Thank you!

Now, there was a pair of doors that the people liked to keep closed, especially when they weren't in the room. Through those doors was the dark room where all of their clothes were. When they were in there, it wasn't dark. But when they left, it usually became dark. They did the same trick as before in our old room. They touched the white stick on the wall. Sometimes, we could slip in there and check it out. If they didn't see us in there, they might close the doors behind one of us. That was prime exploration time. Sometimes we'd be in there for a while. Later, I could hear the man or the woman looking for me. Their sounds would be distant at first, but then closer. Suddenly, the light would come on, the doors swing open; they would see me and let out a startled sound. And I'd calmly walk out. The doors would close behind me, the light would go off, and I could continue going about my business.

One time, after getting locked inside the closet, then being found, I strolled out of the bathroom into the bedroom. I could see Koko, with a smug smile on his face. He knew I was stuck in the closet, but didn't meow or call to me or alert the people. He just laughed and went back to sleep.

But the closet was a lot of fun to explore. It had lots of places to hide, things to smell, other things to smack around and, since it was dark, it was a great place to go when we were scared. The problem was those doors. This is where my brother Apricot comes in. As I may have mentioned, he's a master at opening doors. He's figured out how to reach under the doors and give the right pull and pop open a door. I've tried it, and usually fail. But he just has a gift.

It's gotten easier for him as he's grown up and gotten stronger. He's great at opening the bathroom doors, and especially the closet doors. As we each have grown, we discovered how easy it is to open the closet door. The first time it happened, we were surprised. Apricot and I were rolling around on the floor in the bathroom. As we rolled, we knocked into the closet doors, right in the middle of the two doors. The doors made a squeaking sound and moved a little. We stopped rolling around and stared at the doors. Then Appy pounced on me, and we rolled into the doors again, and they popped open.

Normally, we'd wait till the people were gone, or at least didn't hear our handiwork. Then he'd reach under and pull and pull until it opened. He wasn't always successful, especially when we were younger, but nowadays it's pretty easy.

So we got to spend a lot of time checking out the closet. When we're warm, the closet is a great place to go and cool off. It's dark, cool, and gives us a lot of places to curl up in. Apricot likes to sit out in the open, right in front of the doors. It's like he's their master. The rest of us, we like to find someplace to hide and sleep.

The other thing that Apricot is pretty good at is climbing onto the upper levels of the closet. There are a lot of flat spots that have clothes and other strange things to send down to the floor. There are a lot of interesting things to smell in the closet. The most noticeable things in the closet are clothes that don't smell good. They're usually in large clear crinkly sounding covers. We hate the sound of those crinkly covers moving. But there are other things, like strange animal smells. Some of their shoes smell like strange animals.

One in particular is a favorite of ours. It has lots of fur and is something we like to take out of the closet and wrestle with. We can't help it. I can smell it as soon as I go into the closet. It's on a high level right near the doors. Apricot would try many times to get up there. Finally, after he'd grown more and we could pop open the doors, Appy succeeded in getting to the top level. He'd found the furry shoes and, grabbing one, jumped down to the floor and out the door. There were two of these, and the other one fell onto the floor, right in front of me. It was so indescribable, but I'll give it a try. The first thing that hit me was the color. It had black fur, but, darker than Sabrina's. The next was the smell. It was like something I had smelled only once before, outside, strangely familiar. It was like the rabbit that Momma had told us about. That was it! How strange. And the fur was so soft and smooth. It was strange putting it into my mouth and carrying it, so I just sat there and smelled it.

I heard the man come into the bedroom. He saw Appy and gave out a yell. Appy ran. The man grabbed the furry shoe, the light came on, and he opened the door. And there I was, in the middle of the clothes room, rubbing my face on the furry shoe. He looked at me with a look of surprise, grabbed the shoe, and ushered me out of the room. He closed the door behind me and said something to me. Of course, I ignored it and kept on walking. We would have to get back in there.

One day, while I was sleeping peacefully, the man came over and picked me up. I started to purr. This ended shortly after he handed me over to the mother. But I liked her, too, and I kept on purring. Then he took my front paw and started to push on my paw pad. Naturally, my claws came out. He wasn't intimidated, but rather made a whistling sound and proceeded to bring one of my claws to his other hand. He was holding something shiny. Then he placed my claw and squeezed it. I felt something snip my claw. My sharp claw was gone! It didn't hurt, but it wasn't pleasant either. Before I could react, he'd snipped another. I had had enough of this and tried to leave, but they had me. He snipped the rest of my front claws, then he started on my back claws.

Then, as quickly as he had started, they dropped me. Sabrina, who had come over to see what the fuss was about was next, then Appy. It took them a couple of minutes, but they caught Mickey, too. He started purring loudly. It didn't help him. He got his claws snipped, too. Tigger and Koko also got their claws snipped that day. It felt odd walking around on the stone floor. At least my claws didn't click and give my position away. Excellent! True stealth mode!

I could see my sister licking her paws and pulling at her claws with her teeth. As I slinked down and crept up toward her back, she turned her head and spotted me. I froze, waiting for her to go back to her grooming. One leap turned into a perfect pounce. She jumped and ran away up the stairs. I followed, digging my claws into the soft carpet as I bolted up the stairs after Sabrina. Whoa. So my claws were quiet on the stone and not so helpful on the carpet. This would take some getting used to.

Another of our favorite activities was playing under the man and woman's bed. It was dark, and the bottom of the bed, or the top of our ceiling, was a fluffy dark material that would move if we pushed against it. This was convenient when we rolled around under the bed and needed the room to pin a sibling. Apricot discovered that if he lay on his back, and pulled himself with his nails on the bottom of the bed, he'd really fly. It was awesome!

We'd scoot on our backs from under one side of the bed to the other and back. Soon we were all doing it. And we could keep going around the outside of the bed, along the floor, by digging into the bottom part of the side of the bed. Awesome! We could race and chase each other under and around the bed. We usually didn't do this too much when the people were home.

After a while the material on our ceiling started to tear. Of course, once there was a hole, we had to check it out, then make it bigger. And once it was big enough, we'd go inside the bottom of the bed. It was a heavenly sleep. We were lifted off of the ground, floating just above the floor. There were times that several of us would sleep in there. It was very restful, like floating on air.

One bad thing, there were a lot of springy and pointy metal things in there, too. When the people were on the bed, we'd see the metal things move. We learned how pointy the things were one time, when Mickey and I were wrestling inside the bottom of the bed. One second we were playing, the next he cried out. One of those metal things had poked him in the side of the face. He left some skin and fur inside the bed that day.

Later that day, when the man had seen him hurt, he grabbed him and tried to attack him by rubbing some very smelly water on his wound, then they put some nasty tasting goop on his wound. Poor Mickey. That's what he got for not ducking when I told him to.

As I said, under the bed was a great place to hide, especially when our family let in other people. They would make loud ringing sounds, then one of our human family would open the big front door and let someone into our house. They usually came to look at us. Sometimes the kids would chase us and grab us, and show us to the person. That was scary and we hated it. When that ringing sound happened, we all ran for the bed. Tigger was right behind us. The people who visited our house usually stayed long enough for us to fall asleep under the bed. A lot of times, we would then be woken up by the sound of someone opening our food in the kitchen. This was a good thing. Sometimes it was a false alarm; the man or the woman was making his or her own dinner, but most of the time, I was right. The people do eat some interesting food, especially the meats. Yum! But sometimes their other food smells pretty good, too. This is especially true when we're hungry.

Sabrina has developed a taste for yellow human foods. Usually there's a spare chair at the dinner table for us. That's very respectful of the people to leave that for us. Sabrina likes the little yellow nuggets that look like our crunchy food, but yellow. Whenever they make it, she comes running. The people put a couple of yellow nuggets on the chair next to her. She chows down like she's starving. They always give her more.

The other yellow food she likes is much bigger. I see a bunch of them hanging on one of the flat stone counters. The people grab one of them and put it on the table when they're eating, usually in the morning. For some reason, Sabrina always takes a swipe at the yellow thing, catching it with her nail and dragging it to the ground. I'm not sure why she does that. I know she likes to gnaw on it, but they take it away quickly. And when they break it open, it doesn't smell all that wonderful, kind of like what the people smell like when they come out of the shower.

Me, I like to sit on my perch overlooking the table. I can see my whole family, cat and people; the people sitting around the table eating, my sister or brothers walking nearby waiting for our dinner. And I can check for interesting smells and even look out the window into the back yard. Yes, definitely worth it.

The kitchen has become another favorite place in the house. As we've gotten older, our leaping ability has gotten crazy. All of us can jump from the floor to the counter to the top of the kitchen cabinets, just one sitting cat height below the ceiling. The view is outstanding. Truly makes you feel like the king; or in Sabrina's case, the queen of the house. It was pretty scary the first time I tried it. I jumped from the floor to the counter, no problem. Then I went for the top. I dug my front claws onto the top of the cabinets and had to climb up using my back paws. Thank goodness I exercise. Sabrina and Appy even jump from the counter to the top of the big white cold box, then to the top of the cabinets. On top of the cabinets is one of our favorite spots to sleep. It's warm and safe there. Appy blends in there well. His fur is the same color as the wall. The people don't see him sometimes unless he moves.

Now, for my next trick. Getting to the top of the cabinets is great. Getting to the top of the other cabinets is fun. Only Mickey, Appy, and I have made it. Although Tigger loves to jump to the top of the cabinets, he slowly plops down on the white box, then the counter.

But the real test is the jump. It's about three or four cat lengths from one cabinet top to the other. And there's not a lot of room before we hit the ceiling. The jump requires concentration, poise, and above all else, bravery. The first time the people saw me doing it I almost didn't make it. They almost broke my concentration just as I was jumping. Don't they know that they can't do that to a cat? It's not right. Just as I was springing, I heard them yelling. Thankfully I had judged the distance perfectly and landed right near the edge. I could feel the tips of the fur on my back grazing the ceiling. Cool!

As we've gotten older, and Mickey and Appy have out-grown me, they can make the jump easily, almost without looking. I still have to carefully calibrate myself, then jump. Once, I didn't make it and had to bounce off of the side of the cabinets and land on the counter, then gracefully hit the floor with my paws. I struck a perfect landing.

Of course, like any good cat, when we perfect a new technique, we have to try it out somewhere else. Appy surprised us all one day while we were all in the bathroom. The man was in his litter box looking at us when Appy jumped from the floor onto the big white bowl, then jumped straight up to the top of the shower wall. I could see the satisfied look on his face as he stared down at the rest of us. This was cool! The top of the shower wall was flat, but only one cat-width wide, so he could easily sit and watch us. Since it wasn't too wide, I had to be careful sleeping there. I might end up falling in mid-sleep. This would be unpleasant.

It wasn't long that I gave it a try. I leapt, but didn't make it. Almost. I had to bounce down to the big white bowl, but soon I was on the shower wall. It was very satisfying.

Now Nicholas liked to put a lot of warm water in the big bowl and actually sit in the big bowl. This was the craziest thing we'd ever seen. These people were wild! He actually put on the water, and when there was enough water in there, he would get in and stay there for a while. This was something new, so of course we had to check it out.

This time, Sabrina took the lead. She hopped up to the top of the big white and now wet bowl. It was less than standing on our back paws height, so she could look before she leapt. Once on the bowl, she walked around the bowl to the backside. I could clearly see her moving. Nicholas was splashing water and making the water move. I saw her settle down cautiously in an indent in the bowl, right at the water's edge.

Suddenly the water rose up and splashed her. The surprised look on her face wasn't that of a happy cat. As she started on her way down from the tub, I could see her maneuvering her paws to land the right way. Instead, she landed half on the water's edge and half in the water. I heard scraping of nails on the bowl, I heard clawing and scratching as she stormed out of the water and out of the bathroom. We all ran like the wind after her. Was she all right? What had happened? She was all wet from her belly to her tail. She'd been startled by a splash of water and jumped, but landed with her back paws in the water, while scraping out with her front paws. And when she got all four paws on the ground, she was gone!

So now we have the full run of the house. There are a few doors that we haven't gotten to open yet. Appy is working on it. I have no doubt that we'll crack open Katrina's room and the storage room. There's even a door on the ceiling next to our litter box. I could see Appy hanging from the ceiling someday. That just makes me dizzy thinking about it.

Our history with the man is pretty special and unique. He was the one who took us from our life outside with Momma. He's the one who introduced us to his family, and made us all warm when we're cold and feeds us when we're hungry. We miss Momma, but we miss the man when he's gone, too.

The mother is also warm and caring. One of my first memories with the people is of her holding us keeping us warm, gently talking to us; she knew how sensitive our hearing was; and of falling asleep in her arms.

Katrina was always excited to see us, and I was glad when she chose me to hold over my brothers or sister. She has a spirited personality, always caring and cuddling us. That was a perfect combination to curl up and sleep on.

Nicholas was our first human sleeping buddy. We spent many nights curled on and around him. Even to this day, I like to go up and visit him when he goes to bed. Tigger usually shows up and ruins the fun, but then, he needs a sleeping buddy, too.

One day, when I was sleeping in the sun by the window. Katrina came over to me and picked me up. I like her. She's soft and smells nice. Plus, she knows how to scratch me just right to make me purr. But on this day, she carried me out of the house and into the big metal car. I wasn't happy. She placed me out by the front window. I could see the outside, but couldn't get to it. She started the car and it made a loud rumbling noise and started to shake. This I didn't like at all and started to let her know. I meowed at her as loudly as I could.

She made some movements with her paws and the car started to move. Now I was really scared. What was happening? I meowed and meowed. She kept on driving. I could see people walking along the big white rock that I recognized from when we lived in the cave. So that's what the loud rumbling noise was; people in their cars driving on the big white flat rock. Soon we were back at our house. Katrina stopped the car. She grabbed me and brought me back into the house. I was so happy to be out of that car. But I had learned about the noises from the cave. I found my brothers and sister and told them about my car ride and what I learned. Now, we're a little wary whenever the people pick us up and begin to carry us around. No more car rides for me!

After our evening feeding, the people feed Momma. We like to watch her eat. She sees us through the window, but she seems to be more occupied with eating than watching us. I understand this. I remember eating the food the people put out for us. We were so hungry that we ate the food quickly. Sometimes, when Momma is done eating, she'll stop and look at us. She doesn't stay long after eating and goes off into the bushes. It's almost like she doesn't care about us. After she's gone, we usually pounce on each other or chase one another around the house. Sometimes the people will pick us up and hold us. It's nice to be held at that time. Their warmth and love is satisfying. We return that love whenever we can.

We've become a new family of people and cats. They feed us, care for us, love us, and clean up after us. We love them back, and I think bring them joy. I can see them smiling at us as we come into the room they're in. I can see the man laugh when we play with each other or chase each other around the house. And we like it when they come back home from riding in the car. Sabrina and I will come right over to them, right after Koko. He's annoying, but brave. He's the first one at the door to greet them. I'm learning a lot from him. He's kind of like Mickey and kind of like me. He loves to be with the people, but he doesn't sit on them. Sabrina and I love to sit on the people, stare into their eyes and wonder, "What are they thinking about?" That's another story.

$\mathcal{E}$pilogue

Several years have passed since the time Momma and the kittens came into our lives. The kittens have grown up and are now three years old! Katrina is in college at Texas A&M, and Nicholas is in middle school. I've gotten a new job that requires lots of travel. But I'm not complaining. Monica is exploring ways to advance her career.

Our beloved Koko has passed away. During the time I was writing this book, he developed stomach cancer. He stopped eating and eventually had to be put to sleep. He's sorely missed. Tigger is stuck dealing with the ever-present kittens, and he hasn't lost any weight. I'll bet he's still thanking me everyday for bringing them into our house.

Patches and Sabrina have become the consummate lap cats who hang on us whenever they feel like it. Appy is just Appy. He's a lover, not a fighter. He loves us, is always there for dinner or breakfast, and absolutely loves to open doors, climb on our kitchen cabinets, or any high place he can find and he still delivers his love nibbles. Mickey is so cute. His pink nose is adorable. He'll gently rub against my feet as I ready their meals. He's still shy, but allows us to grab him occasionally. And when we do grab him, he purrs like crazy. He's the biggest of the cats and has the highest pitch meow of all of them. It's pretty funny. We call it his squirrely meow. He's slowly starting to come out of his shell.

Momma still lives outside and refuses to come into the house. We feed her every day. She still hisses at me, then gives me a gentle meow. We did catch her and have her spayed, but as Nicholas reminds me, not soon enough.

The story doesn't end here. Before we had her spayed, Momma had another litter. Her sole surviving kitten's name is Squirt. She's a carbon copy of Sabrina. She's gotten pretty close to Mickey. They look really cute sleeping together! She's in the house with us. And she has quite a story to tell!

About the Authors

Alex grew up on Long Island, NY with a menagerie of pets, including cats, a mongoose, and a raccoon. Growing up in a family of animal lovers led Alex to have a strong compassion and love for all animals. He lives in Flower Mound, TX with his wife Monica, and their two children, Katrina and Nicholas, and seven cats. When Alex isn't caring for the cats he enjoys family outings and camping with his son's Boy Scout troop. Alex has an entrepreneurial spirit and has tried several startup businesses. He's the designer and publisher of an iPhone app called POTUS, Commander-in-Chief, a role-playing game.

Patches was born and raised in Flower Mound, TX. He has two brothers and one sister. Having a short, but exciting feral life, Patches has acquiesced to the gentle country living those large suburban, planned communities in North Texas offer. After being adopted by his new family, Patches and his brothers and sister live a normal indoor feline existence focused on maximizing the entertainment value provided by their new family and of course by gravity.

Patches loves to explore, stalk, and pounce on any family member who's an unwitting assistant. Sometimes, he becomes the hunted, but this is rare. He likes the sun, a warm bed, and someone to sit on.

You can find videos, pictures and other links on our website: http://www.theflowofkittens.com

And on YouTube on the Flow of Kittens channel. And you can like us on Facebook.

Kitten Nicknames

Real name	Patches	Sabrina	Apricot	Mickey
Original name	Patches	Venom	Lilly	Hissy
Most common	Patchy	Brini	Appy	Mickles
Fun name		Denise*	l'orange	

As a group, sometimes I call them the horde, the flow, or the kittens, depending on their arrival technique. *Sabrina earned another nickname, Denise. In Russian the word Vniece means "down," as in the directive "Get Down!" I typically would direct that comment at a cat that comes up onto the kitchen table. It's usually ignored. The kids have absorbed that as "Denise," after a good family friend, Denise Trafas, so it's not uncommon to hear Nicholas yelling at Sabrina "Denise." It might go something like this. "Sabrina, Denise." That's how she earned the middle name, "Sabrina Denise Zekulin." It's now her official middle name at the vet.

Made in the USA
Lexington, KY
04 December 2012